100 Calorie
SNACKS & MORE

Publications International, Ltd.

Pictured on the front cover *(clockwise from top left):* Caribbean Chutney Kabobs *(page 68),* Raspberry Smoothies *(page 130),* Mediterranean Pita Pizzas *(page 54)* and New Wave Chicken Salad Wraps *(page 58).*
Pictured on the back cover *(top to bottom):* Watermelon Granita *(page 6),* Tropical Sugar Cookie Bars *(page 48)* and Wild Wedges *(page 76).*

ISBN-13: 978-1-4508-4001-9
ISBN-10: 1-4508-4001-9

Library of Congress Control Number: 20011915924

Manufactured in China.

8 7 6 5 4 3 2 1

Nutritional Analysis: Every effort has been made to check the accuracy of the nutritional information that appears with each recipe. However, because numerous variables account for a wide range of values for certain foods, nutritive analyses in this book should be considered approximate. Different results may be obtained by using different nutrient databases and different brand-name products.

Microwave Cooking: Microwave ovens vary in wattage. Use the cooking times as guidelines and check for doneness before adding more time.

Note: This book is for informational purposes and is not intended to provide medical advice. Neither Publications International, Ltd., nor the authors, editors or publisher takes responsibility for any possible consequences from any treatment, procedure, exercise, dietary modification, action, or applications of medication or preparation by any person reading or following the information in this cookbook. The publication of this book does not constitute the practice of medicine, and this cookbook does not replace your physician, pharmacist or health-care specialist. **Before undertaking any course of treatment or nutritional plan, the authors, editors and publisher advise the reader to check with a physician or other health-care provider.**

Publications International, Ltd.

Contents

·Sweet· Treats

Banana and Ginger Cream Mousse

1 teaspoon unflavored gelatin
¼ cup fat-free half-and-half
2 tablespoons (½ ounce) finely chopped crystallized ginger
1 cup thawed reduced-fat whipped topping
1 large banana, thinly sliced
1 whole low-fat graham cracker, crushed

1. Sprinkle gelatin over half-and-half in medium bowl. Let stand 5 minutes or until gelatin softens. Stir in ginger; fold in whipped topping. Chill 1 hour or until firm but not stiff.

2. Gently stir ginger cream. Divide among four dessert bowls. Top each with one fourth of banana slices and one fourth of cracker crumbs. Serve immediately.

Makes 4 servings

Nutrients per Serving: Calories: 90, Calories from Fat: 30%, Total Fat: 3g, Saturated Fat: 3g, Cholesterol: 0mg, Sodium: 40mg, Carbohydrate: 16g, Fiber: 1g, Protein: 2g

• Sweet **Treats** •

Watermelon Granita

5 cups cubed seeded watermelon
¹/₂ cup sugar
1 envelope (¹/₄ ounce) unflavored gelatin
¹/₂ cup cranberry juice cocktail

1. Process watermelon in food processor until nearly smooth. (You should have about 3¹/₃ cups.)

2. Combine sugar and gelatin in small saucepan. Gradually stir in juice. Cook and stir over low heat until gelatin dissolves. Add to watermelon purée in food processor; process until combined. Pour into 8-inch square baking dish. Cover and freeze about 5 hours or until firm.

3. Break watermelon mixture into chunks in baking dish. Freeze about 3 hours or until firm. To serve, stir and scrape granita with fork to create icy texture. Spoon into dessert dishes. *Makes 8 servings*

Nutrients per Serving (¹/₂ cup): Calories: 88, Calories from Fat: 0%, Total Fat: 0g, Saturated Fat: 0g, Cholesterol: 0mg, Sodium: 5mg, Carbohydrate: 22g, Fiber: <1g, Protein: 1g

Citrus Fruit Toss

¹/₄ cup dried cranberries
¹/₄ cup water
2 cups red grapefruit sections, drained
2 tablespoons sucralose-based sugar substitute
2 tablespoons fresh mint leaves, chopped
1 tablespoon lime juice

1. Combine cranberries and water in medium microwavable bowl. Microwave on HIGH 1 minute; let stand 5 minutes. Drain well.

2. Combine cranberries, grapefruit, sugar substitute, mint and lime juice in same bowl; toss gently. Let stand 5 minutes before serving. *Makes 4 servings*

Nutrients per Serving (¹/₂ cup): Calories: 74, Calories from Fat: 2%, Total Fat: <1g, Saturated Fat: <1g, Cholesterol: 0mg, Sodium: <1mg, Carbohydrate: 20g, Fiber: 2g, Protein: <1g

Watermelon Granita

Peach Turnovers

2 cups chopped peeled fresh peaches or frozen unsweetened peach slices, thawed, drained and chopped
2 tablespoons granulated sugar
1 tablespoon all-purpose flour
¹⁄₄ teaspoon vanilla
¹⁄₈ teaspoon ground nutmeg
6 sheets (about 12×8¹⁄₄ inches each) frozen phyllo dough, thawed
 Nonstick cooking spray
1 tablespoon powdered sugar

1. Preheat oven to 375°F. Line baking sheet with parchment paper or foil. Combine peaches, granulated sugar, flour, vanilla and nutmeg in medium bowl; toss until combined.

2. Place one sheet phyllo dough on damp kitchen towel. (Keep remaining dough covered.) Lightly spray dough with cooking spray. Top with second sheet phyllo. Using sharp knife or pizza cutter, cut into two lengthwise strips, each about 12×4 inches.

3. For each turnover, spoon about ¹⁄₃ cup peach mixture onto dough about 1 inch from end of each strip. Fold one corner over filling to make triangle. Continue folding as you would fold a flag to form triangle that encloses filling. Repeat with remaining dough and filling. Place on prepared baking sheet. Spray tops of turnovers with cooking spray.

4. Bake about 17 minutes or until golden brown. Cool on wire rack 10 minutes. Sprinkle with powdered sugar. Serve warm. *Makes 6 servings*

....

Nutrients per Serving: Calories: 103, Calories from Fat: 8%, Total Fat: 1g, Saturated Fat: <1g, Cholesterol: 0mg, Sodium: 92mg, Carbohydrate: 21g, Fiber: 1g, Protein: 2g

• Sweet **Treats** •

Chocolate Cream Dessert Dip

2 cups fat-free (skim) milk
1 package (4-serving size) chocolate fat-free sugar-free instant pudding and pie filling mix
1 container (8 ounces) thawed fat-free whipped topping
2 tablespoons chocolate chips, finely chopped
   Chocolate curls (optional)

Beat milk and pudding mix in medium bowl with electric mixer at medium speed 2 minutes. Stir in whipped topping and chocolate chips until well blended. Refrigerate until ready to serve. Garnish with chocolate curls. *Makes 24 servings*

Nutrients per Serving (2 tablespoons dip without fruit): Calories: 33, Calories from Fat: 9%, Total Fat: <1g, Saturated Fat: <1g, Cholesterol: <1mg, Sodium: 38mg, Carbohydrate: 6g, Fiber: 0g, Protein: <1g

Choco-Cherry Chill

62 calories

1 can (about 14 ounces) pitted tart cherries in water, undrained
1½ cups frozen pitted unsweetened dark Bing cherries
1 cup fat-free half-and-half
½ cup reduced-sugar chocolate syrup
1 teaspoon vanilla
   Fresh mint leaves (optional)
   Additional frozen cherries (optional)

1. Place tart cherries with liquid, Bing cherries, half-and-half, chocolate syrup and vanilla in blender; blend until smooth.

2. Freeze cherry mixture in ice cream maker according to manufacturer's directions.

3. Let stand 15 minutes at room temperature before serving. Garnish each serving with mint and additional cherry. *Makes 8 servings*

Nutrients per Serving (½ cup): Calories: 62, Calories from Fat: 2%, Total Fat: <1g, Saturated Fat: <1g, Cholesterol: 4mg, Sodium: 41mg, Carbohydrate: 14g, Fiber: 1g, Protein: 2g

Chocolate Cream Dessert Dip

• Sweet **Treats** •

Cheesecake Bites with Ginger-Berry Topping

8 gingersnap cookies (2-inch diameter)

4 ounces fat-free cream cheese, softened

1 package (4-serving size) cheesecake-flavored fat-free sugar-free instant pudding and pie filling mix

1¼ cups fat-free (skim) milk

Ginger-Berry Topping

½ cup sugar-free blueberry preserves

¾ cup fresh or thawed frozen blueberries

1 teaspoon ground ginger

1. Line 24 mini (1¾-inch) muffin cups with paper baking cups. Break gingersnaps into pieces; process in food processor to make about ½ cup fine crumbs. Place 1 teaspoon crumbs in each cup.

2. Beat cream cheese in medium bowl with electric mixer at low speed until smooth. Add pudding mix and milk; beat at high speed 2 minutes or until smooth and creamy. Spoon rounded tablespoonful cream cheese mixture into each cup. Place pan in freezer while preparing topping.

3. For Ginger-Berry Topping, place preserves in medium microwavable bowl. Microwave on HIGH 15 seconds. Stir in blueberries and ginger.

4. Spoon 1 teaspoon topping over each cheesecake bite. Serve immediately or cover and refrigerate up to 2 hours. *Makes 8 servings*

Nutrients per Serving (3 pieces): Calories: 87, Calories from Fat: 10%, Total Fat: 1g, Saturated Fat: 0g, Cholesterol: 2mg, Sodium: 305mg, Carbohydrate: 18g, Fiber: 1g, Protein: 4g

Cheesecake Bites with Ginger-Berry Topping

Sweet **Treats**

Grapefruit Sorbet

1 large pink grapefruit
¹⁄₂ cup apple juice
1¹⁄₂ tablespoons sugar

1. Peel grapefruit and remove white pith. Cut into segments over bowl to catch juices, removing membranes between segments. Combine grapefruit, grapefruit juice, apple juice and sugar in food processor or blender; process until smooth.

2. Freeze grapefruit mixture in ice cream maker according to manufacturer's directions. Serve immediately. *Makes 4 servings*

Nutrients per Serving (¹⁄₃ cup): Calories: 59, Calories from Fat: 0%, Total Fat: 0g, Saturated Fat: 0g, Cholesterol: 0mg, Sodium: 0mg, Carbohydrate: 15g, Fiber: 1g, Protein: <1g

Baked Pear Dessert

¹⁄₃ cup unsweetened apple cider or apple juice, divided
2 tablespoons dried cranberries or raisins
1 tablespoon toasted sliced almonds
¹⁄₈ teaspoon ground cinnamon
1 medium unpeeled pear (about 6 ounces), cut in half lengthwise and cored
¹⁄₂ cup vanilla low-fat sugar-free ice cream or frozen yogurt

1. Preheat oven to 350°F. Combine 1 tablespoon cider, cranberries, almonds and cinnamon in small bowl.

2. Place pear halves, cut sides up, in small baking dish. Evenly mound almond mixture on top of pear halves. Pour remaining cider into dish around pear halves; cover with foil.

3. Bake 35 to 40 minutes or until pears are soft, spooning cider in dish over pears once or twice during baking. Serve warm with ice cream. *Makes 2 servings*

Nutrients per Serving (1 pear half with ¹⁄₄ cup ice cream): Calories: 87, Calories from Fat: 19%, Total Fat: 2g, Saturated Fat: <1g, Cholesterol: 3mg, Sodium: 13mg, Carbohydrate: 16g, Fiber: 1g, Protein: 1g

Grapefruit Sorbet

• Sweet **Treats** •

Strawberry and Peach Crisp

1 cup frozen unsweetened peach slices, thawed and cut into 1-inch pieces
1 cup sliced fresh strawberries
3 teaspoons sugar, divided
1/4 cup bran cereal flakes
2 tablespoons old-fashioned oats
1 tablespoon all-purpose flour
1/8 teaspoon ground cinnamon
1/8 teaspoon salt
2 teaspoons unsalted margarine, cut into small pieces

1. Preheat oven to 325°F. Spray 1- to 1½-quart baking dish with nonstick cooking spray.

2. Combine peaches and strawberries in medium bowl. Sprinkle with 1 teaspoon sugar. Transfer fruit to prepared baking dish.

3. Combine cereal, oats, flour, cinnamon and salt in small bowl. Stir in remaining 2 teaspoons sugar. Add margarine; stir with fork until mixture resembles coarse crumbs. Sprinkle over fruit in baking dish.

4. Bake 20 minutes or until fruit is hot and topping is slightly browned.

Makes 4 servings

Variation: Substitute 2 teaspoons packed brown sugar for the 2 teaspoons granulated sugar in the topping.

Variation: For a strawberry crisp, omit the peaches and use 2 cups strawberries in the recipe.

Nutrients per Serving (1/2 cup): Calories: 80, Calories from Fat: 24%, Total Fat: 2g, Saturated Fat: <1g, Cholesterol: 0mg, Sodium: 83mg, Carbohydrate: 15g, Fiber: 3g, Protein: 1g

Chocolate Chip Frozen Yogurt

1 cup plain fat-free yogurt
1/2 cup fat-free half-and-half
2 tablespoons sugar
1/4 teaspoon vanilla
1/4 cup mini chocolate chips

1. Combine yogurt, half-and-half, sugar and vanilla in medium bowl; mix well.

2. Freeze yogurt mixture in ice cream maker according to manufacturer's directions until soft. Add chocolate chips; freeze until firm. *Makes 6 servings*

Nutrients per Serving (1/3 cup): Calories: 87, Calories from Fat: 21%, Total Fat: 2g, Saturated Fat: 1g, Cholesterol: 4mg, Sodium: 52mg, Carbohydrate: 14g, Fiber: <1g, Protein: 3g

Berries with Creamy Lemon Ricotta

110 calories

12 ounces (about 1 1/2 cups) reduced-fat ricotta cheese
3 tablespoons sugar
1 teaspoon grated lemon peel, plus additional for garnish
2 tablespoons lemon juice
1 teaspoon vanilla
2 cups fresh blueberries and/or raspberries

1. Stir ricotta, sugar, 1 teaspoon lemon peel, lemon juice and vanilla in medium bowl until well blended. Cover and refrigerate up to 2 hours.

2. Spoon ricotta mixture into six dessert dishes. Top with berries and garnish with additional lemon peel. *Makes 6 servings*

Nutrients per Serving (1/3 cup ricotta mixture with 1/3 cup berries): Calories: 110, Calories from Fat: 25%, Total Fat: 3g, Saturated Fat: 2g, Cholesterol: 18mg, Sodium: 138mg, Carbohydrate: 17g, Fiber: 1g, Protein: 7g

Chocolate Chip Frozen Yogurt

Summer Strawberry Orange Cups

2 cups fresh strawberries, divided
1 envelope (¹/₄ ounce) unflavored gelatin
2 tablespoons cold water
2 tablespoons boiling water
1¹/₂ cups reduced-fat (2%) milk
¹/₂ cup frozen orange juice concentrate
1 teaspoon vanilla
Fresh mint leaves (optional)

1. Cut 1 cup strawberries into thin slices; place in bottom of six 8-ounce dessert dishes or custard cups.

2. Combine gelatin and cold water in small bowl; let stand 5 minutes. Add boiling water; stir until gelatin is completely dissolved.

3. Combine milk, orange juice concentrate and vanilla in medium bowl; mix well. Let stand at room temperature 20 minutes. Stir in gelatin mixture until well blended. Pour evenly over sliced strawberries in dishes. Refrigerate 2 hours or until completely set.

4. Slice remaining 1 cup strawberries; arrange on top of each dessert. Garnish with mint.   *Makes 6 servings*

Nutrients per Serving: Calories: 89, Calories from Fat: 10%, Total Fat: 1g, Saturated Fat: <1g, Cholesterol: 5mg, Sodium: 29mg, Carbohydrate: 16g, Fiber: 1g, Protein: 4g

• Sweet **Treats** •

Mango Mousse

1 **envelope (¹⁄₄ ounce) unflavored gelatin**
¹⁄₂ **cup cold water**
¹⁄₂ **cup boiling water**
2¹⁄₂ **cups mango chunks (see Note), plus additional for garnish**
2 **tablespoons sugar**
2 **teaspoons lemon juice**
³⁄₄ **cup thawed fat-free whipped topping, divided**

1. Combine gelatin and cold water in small bowl; let stand 5 minutes. Add boiling water; stir until gelatin is completely dissolved. Set aside to cool.

2. Combine 2¹⁄₂ cups mango, sugar and lemon juice in blender or food processor; blend until smooth. Spoon mango mixture into large bowl; stir in gelatin mixture. Gently fold in ¹⁄₂ cup whipped topping. Refrigerate 1 hour or until firm.

3. Spoon into eight dessert cups. Top each serving with 1¹⁄₂ teaspoons whipped topping. Garnish with additional mango chunks. *Makes 8 servings*

Note: Use 2 medium or large fresh mangos or a 1-pound package of frozen mango chunks packed without sugar. Measure out 2¹⁄₂ cups.

Nutrients per Serving (¹⁄₃ cup): Calories: 70, Calories from Fat: 0%, Total Fat: 0g, Saturated Fat: 0g, Cholesterol: 0mg, Sodium: 3mg, Carbohydrate: 17g, Fiber: 1g, Protein: 1g

 Tip Cutting a mango requires cutting around the large flat seed that runs the length of the fruit. Place the mango, stem side down, on a cutting board with the narrow end facing you. Cut through the rounded sides about ¹⁄₄ inch from the top center. With the peel still on, cut parallel slices into the fruit of the rounded sides, then scoop out the slices with a spoon.

Mango Mousse

• Sweet **Treats** •

Peaches with Raspberry Sauce

1 cup fresh raspberries
¹/₂ cup water
¹/₄ cup sugar substitute
6 fresh peach halves
¹/₃ cup vanilla fat-free yogurt

1. Combine raspberries, water and sugar substitute in small saucepan. Bring to a boil over medium-high heat, stirring frequently. Boil 1 minute. Transfer to food processor or blender; process until smooth. Set aside 15 minutes to cool.

2. Drizzle ¹/₄ cup raspberry sauce onto each of six serving dishes. Place one peach half on each dish. Spoon about 2¹/₂ teaspoons yogurt over each peach half.

Makes 6 servings

Nutrients per Serving (1 peach half with ¹/₄ cup raspberry sauce and about 2¹/₂ teaspoons yogurt): Calories: 41, Calories from Fat: 0%, Total Fat: 0g, Saturated Fat: 0g, Cholesterol: <1mg, Sodium: 9mg, Carbohydrate: 10g, Fiber: 2g, Protein: 1g

Strawberries with Honeyed Yogurt Sauce

1 cup plain low-fat yogurt
1 tablespoon orange juice
1 to 2 teaspoons honey
  Ground cinnamon
1 quart fresh strawberries, stems removed

Combine yogurt, juice, honey and cinnamon to taste in small bowl; mix well. Serve sauce over strawberries.

Makes 4 servings

Nutrients per Serving (1 cup strawberries with about ¹/₄ cup sauce): Calories: 88, Calories from Fat: 10%, Total Fat: 1g, Saturated Fat: 1g, Cholesterol: 4mg, Sodium: 41mg, Carbohydrate: 16g, Fiber: 4g, Protein: 4g

Peaches with Raspberry Sauce

Sweet Treats

Mocha Cream Tartlets

**1 package (4-serving size) chocolate fat-free sugar-free cook-and-serve
pudding and pie filling mix**
2 cups fat-free half-and-half, divided
1 1/2 teaspoons instant coffee granules
1/8 teaspoon ground cinnamon
1/2 cup old-fashioned oats
1/2 cup all-purpose flour
1/4 cup graham cracker crumbs
1 tablespoon sugar
1/4 cup unsalted margarine, melted
1 1/2 cups thawed reduced-fat whipped topping
16 chocolate-covered espresso beans (optional)

1. Combine pudding mix and 1/2 cup half-and-half in medium saucepan; stir until smooth. Stir in remaining 1 1/2 cups half-and-half, coffee and cinnamon. Bring to a boil over medium-high heat, stirring constantly. Remove from heat; spoon into medium bowl and refrigerate at least 1 hour.

2. Preheat oven to 375°F. Line 16 standard (2 1/2-inch) muffin cups with paper baking cups.

3. Combine oats, flour, cracker crumbs and sugar in medium bowl. Stir in margarine until mixture comes together when pressed. Spoon 1 tablespoon crumb mixture into each cup; press to form crust. Bake 13 minutes or until crusts are golden brown and firm. Cool completely in pan on wire rack.

4. To assemble tartlets, gently fold whipped topping into chocolate pudding. Spoon mixture into cooled crusts. Garnish with espresso beans.   *Makes 16 servings*

Note: The filling in the tartlets may be soft or firm depending on the pudding mix. For a firmer filling, chill the assembled tartlets for 2 or more hours.

Nutrients per Serving (1 tartlet): Calories: 100, Calories from Fat: 45%, Total Fat: 5g, Saturated Fat: 2g, Cholesterol: 0mg, Sodium: 70mg, Carbohydrate: 13g, Fiber: 0g, Protein: 2g

• Sweet **Treats** •

Citrus Tapioca Pudding

2 navel oranges
2½ cups fat-free (skim) milk
⅓ cup sugar
¼ cup cholesterol-free egg substitute
3 tablespoons quick-cooking tapioca
½ teaspoon almond extract
    Ground cinnamon or nutmeg
    Orange slices (optional)

1. Grate peel of 1 orange into medium saucepan. Add milk, sugar, egg substitute and tapioca; let stand 5 minutes. Cook and stir over medium heat 5 minutes or until mixture comes to a boil. Remove from heat; stir in almond extract. Let stand 20 minutes. Stir well; cool to room temperature. Cover and refrigerate at least 2 hours.

2. Peel and dice oranges. Stir tapioca mixture; fold in oranges. Spoon into eight dessert dishes. Sprinkle each serving with cinnamon; garnish with orange slices.

Makes 8 servings

Nutrients per Serving: Calories: 89, Calories from Fat: 2%, Total Fat: <1g, Saturated Fat: <1g, Cholesterol: 1mg, Sodium: 50mg, Carbohydrate: 19g, Fiber: 1g, Protein: 4g

Cantaloupe Sorbet

6 cups cubed fresh cantaloupe
⅓ cup light corn syrup
3 tablespoons lime juice

1. Process cantaloupe in food processor until puréed. (You should have about 3 cups.) Add corn syrup and lime juice; process until combined.

2. Freeze cantaloupe mixture in ice cream maker according to manufacturer's directions.

Makes 8 servings

Nutrients per Serving (½ cup): Calories: 103, Calories from Fat: 0%, Total Fat: 0g, Saturated Fat: 0g, Cholesterol: 0mg, Sodium: 29mg, Carbohydrate: 26g, Fiber: 1g, Protein: 2g

·Cookies,·
Bars & Bites

Angelic Macaroons

1 package (16 ounces) angel food cake mix
¹/₂ cup cold water
1 teaspoon almond extract
1 package (14 ounces) sweetened flaked coconut
¹/₂ cup slivered almonds, coarsley chopped

1. Preheat oven to 325°F. Line cookie sheets with parchment paper.

2. Beat cake mix, water and almond extract in large bowl with electric mixer at medium speed until well blended. Add half of coconut; beat until blended. Add remaining coconut and almonds; beat until well blended. Drop dough by tablespoonfuls about 2 inches apart onto prepared cookie sheets.

3. Bake 22 to 25 minutes or until golden brown. Cool cookies on cookie sheets 3 minutes. Remove to wire racks; cool completely. *Makes 40 cookies*

Nutrients per Serving (1 cookie): Calories: 94, Calories from Fat: 38%, Total Fat: 4g, Saturated Fat: 3g, Cholesterol: 0mg, Sodium: 86mg, Carbohydrate: 14g, Fiber: 1g, Protein: 2g

Cookies, **Bars & Bites**

S'more Treats

2¹/₂ cups cocoa-flavored sweetened rice cereal
6 whole low-fat honey graham crackers
3 tablespoons margarine
1 tablespoon sucralose-brown sugar blend
3¹/₂ cups mini marshmallows, divided
1 square (1 ounce) semisweet or milk chocolate, melted (optional)

1. Lightly spray 9-inch square baking pan with nonstick cooking spray. Place cereal in large bowl. Crumble graham crackers into ¹/₄-inch pieces; add to bowl. Toss to combine.

2. Combine margarine and sucralose-brown sugar blend in large microwavable bowl; microwave on HIGH 25 to 30 seconds or until margarine is melted. Add 2¹/₂ cups marshmallows; microwave on HIGH 1¹/₂ to 2 minutes or until marshmallows are melted, stirring after 1 minute. Stir until mixture is smooth.

3. Add marshmallow mixture to cereal mixture; stir to coat. Add remaining 1 cup marshmallows; stir until blended. Press evenly into prepared pan using waxed paper. Cool completely. Drizzle with chocolate, if desired. Cut into squares.

Makes 16 squares

Nutrients per Serving (1 square): Calories: 89, Calories from Fat: 20%, Total Fat: 2g, Saturated Fat: <1g, Cholesterol: 0mg, Sodium: 79mg, Carbohydrate: 16g, Fiber: 0g, Protein: <1g

Tip For a slightly thicker treat, use an 8-inch square baking pan. Or for some variety, cut out fun shapes using a greased 2-inch cookie cutter.

Cinnamon Flats

1³/₄ cups all-purpose flour
¹/₂ cup sugar
1¹/₂ teaspoons ground cinnamon
¹/₄ teaspoon salt
¹/₄ teaspoon ground nutmeg
¹/₂ cup (1 stick) cold margarine
3 egg whites, divided
1 teaspoon vanilla
1 teaspoon water
Sugar Glaze (recipe follows)

1. Preheat oven to 350°F. Spray 15×10-inch jelly-roll pan with nonstick cooking spray. Combine flour, sugar, cinnamon, salt and nutmeg in medium bowl. Cut in margarine with pastry blender or two knives until mixture forms coarse crumbs. Beat in 2 egg whites and vanilla; mix to form soft dough.

2. Divide dough into six equal pieces; place on prepared pan. Press dough evenly to edges of pan; smooth top of dough with spatula. Mix remaining egg white and water in small cup; brush over dough. Lightly score dough into 2×1¹/₂-inch pieces.

3. Bake 20 to 25 minutes or until lightly browned and firm. While still warm, cut along score lines into pieces; drizzle with Sugar Glaze. Let stand 15 minutes or until glaze is firm before removing from pan. *Makes 50 cookies*

Sugar Glaze

1¹/₂ cups powdered sugar
2 to 3 tablespoons fat-free (skim) milk
1 teaspoon vanilla

Combine sugar, 2 tablespoons milk and vanilla in small bowl. If glaze is too thick, add remaining 1 tablespoon milk. *Makes about ³/₄ cup*

Nutrients per Serving (1 cookie): Calories: 48, Calories from Fat: 18%, Total Fat: 1g, Saturated Fat: <1g, Cholesterol: <1mg, Sodium: 35mg, Carbohydrate: 9g, Fiber: <1g, Protein: 1g

• Cookies, **Bars & Bites** •

Cocoa-Almond Meringue Puffs

2 tablespoons granulated sugar
3 packets sugar substitute
1 1/2 teaspoons unsweetened cocoa powder
2 egg whites, at room temperature
1/2 teaspoon vanilla
1/4 teaspoon cream of tartar
1/4 teaspoon almond extract
1/8 teaspoon salt
1 1/2 ounces (7 tablespoons) sliced almonds
3 tablespoons seedless raspberry fruit spread

1. Preheat oven to 275°F. Line cookie sheet with foil. Combine granulated sugar, sugar substitute and cocoa in small bowl.

2. Beat egg whites in medium bowl with electric mixer at high speed until foamy. Add vanilla, cream of tartar, almond extract and salt; beat until soft peaks form. Add sugar mixture, 1 tablespoon at a time, beating until stiff peaks form.

3. Spoon 15 equal mounds egg white mixture onto prepared cookie sheet. Sprinkle with almonds.

4. Bake 1 hour. Turn oven off but do not open door. Leave cookies in oven 2 hours or until completely dry. Remove from oven; cool completely.

5. Spoon about 1/2 teaspoon fruit spread onto each cookie just before serving.

Makes 15 cookies

Tip: These cookies are best if eaten the same day they're made. If necessary, store them in an airtight container, adding the fruit spread just before serving.

Nutrients per Serving (1 cookie): Calories: 34, Calories from Fat: 26%, Total Fat: 1g, Saturated Fat: <1g, Cholesterol: 0mg, Sodium: 27mg, Carbohydrate: 5g, Fiber: <1g, Protein: 1g

Cookies, **Bars & Bites**

Lemon Almond Biscotti

⅓ cup margarine, softened
⅔ cup sugar
 2 tablespoons grated lemon peel
 1 teaspoon baking powder
½ teaspoon baking soda
⅛ teaspoon salt
 2 eggs
2½ cups all-purpose flour
½ cup slivered almonds

1. Preheat oven to 375°F. Beat margarine in large bowl with electric mixer at medium speed 30 seconds. Add sugar, lemon peel, baking powder, baking soda and salt; beat until well blended. Beat in eggs. Add flour; beat until crumbly. (Dough will be fairly dry.) Stir in almonds.

2. Shape dough into two 9-inch logs. Flatten logs to 1½-inch thickness. Place on nonstick cookie sheet.

3. Bake 20 minutes or until toothpick inserted into centers of logs comes out clean. Cool on cookie sheet 1 hour.

4. Cut each log crosswise into 16 (½-inch) slices. Place slices, cut side down, on cookie sheet; bake 8 minutes. Turn and bake 8 minutes or until crisp and golden. Cool completely on wire racks. Store in airtight container up to 3 days.

Makes 32 biscotti

Nutrients per Serving (1 biscotti): Calories: 85, Calories from Fat: 35%, Total Fat: 3g, Saturated Fat: <1g, Cholesterol: 13mg, Sodium: 70mg, Carbohydrate: 12g, Fiber: <1g, Protein: 2g

Lemon Almond Biscotti

Raspberry Oat Bars

    1 cup old-fashioned oats
$^1/_2$ cup all-purpose flour
$^1/_2$ cup soy-protein cereal clusters
    2 tablespoons sugar
$^1/_4$ teaspoon ground cinnamon
$^1/_8$ teaspoon salt
    5 tablespoons margarine, cut into small pieces
$^3/_4$ cup raspberry fruit spread

1. Preheat oven to 350°F. Spray 8-inch square baking pan with nonstick cooking spray.

2. Combine oats, flour, cereal, sugar, cinnamon and salt in food processor; process until blended. Add margarine; process with on/off pulses just until coarse crumbs form. Set aside $^1/_2$ cup crumbs for topping. Press remaining crumbs onto bottom of prepared pan.

3. Bake 15 minutes. Spread fruit spread over crust; sprinkle with reserved crumbs. Bake 20 to 25 minutes or until edges are browned and fruit spread is firm. Cool slightly in pan on wire rack. Cut into bars. *Makes 20 bars*

Nutrients per Serving (1 bar): Calories: 80, Calories from Fat: 34%, Total Fat: 3g, Saturated Fat: <1g, Cholesterol: 0mg, Sodium: 50mg, Carbohydrate: 13g, Fiber: 1g, Protein: 1g

Raspberry Oat Bars

• Cookies, **Bars & Bites** •

Apple & Raisin Softies

1^3/$_4$ cups all-purpose flour
^{1}/$_2$ cup whole wheat flour
1^1/$_2$ teaspoons pumpkin pie spice
^{1}/$_2$ teaspoon baking soda
^{1}/$_2$ teaspoon baking powder
^{3}/$_4$ cup (1^1/$_2$ sticks) margarine, softened
^{3}/$_4$ cup packed sucralose-brown sugar blend
1 egg
^{1}/$_2$ cup unsweetened applesauce
1 small apple, peeled, cored and finely chopped
1 cup walnuts, chopped
^{3}/$_4$ cup raisins

1. Preheat oven to 375°F. Line cookie sheets with parchment paper. Combine all-purpose flour, whole wheat flour, pumpkin pie spice, baking soda and baking powder in medium bowl.

2. Beat margarine and sucralose-brown sugar blend in large bowl with electric mixer at medium speed until blended. Add egg; beat until blended. Stir in applesauce. Gradually add flour mixture; beat until well blended. Stir in apple, walnuts and raisins.

3. Drop dough by tablespoonfuls about 2 inches apart onto prepared cookie sheets. Gently flatten with back of spoon.

4. Bake 14 to 16 minutes or until deep golden brown. Cool cookies on cookie sheets 5 minutes. Remove to wire racks; cool completely.   *Makes 36 cookies*

Nutrients per Serving (1 cookie): Calories: 107, Calories from Fat: 50%, Total Fat: 6g, Saturated Fat: 1g, Cholesterol: 6mg, Sodium: 71mg, Carbohydrate: 12g, Fiber: 1g, Protein: 2g

• Cookies, **Bars & Bites** •

Pistachio Pinwheels

1 package (8 ounces) reduced-fat cream cheese, softened
1/2 cup (1 stick) soft baking butter with canola oil
2 cups all-purpose flour
3 tablespoons apricot fruit spread
1 tablespoon water
2 tablespoons sugar
1/4 teaspoon ground cinnamon
1/2 cup finely chopped pistachios, toasted*
Nonstick cooking spray

*To toast nuts, spread in single layer on baking sheet. Bake in preheated 350°F oven 5 to 7 minutes or until golden brown, stirring frequently.

1. Preheat oven to 350°F. Line cookie sheets with parchment paper.

2. Beat cream cheese in large bowl with electric mixer at low speed 30 seconds or until smooth. Beat in butter until well blended. Add flour in three batches, beating at low speed until blended. Divide dough into two equal portions; shape into rectangles. Wrap in plastic wrap; refrigerate 20 minutes.

3. Stir fruit spread and water in small bowl. Combine sugar and cinnamon in another small bowl.

4. Roll out each piece of dough into 12×10-inch rectangle on lightly floured surface. Spread 2 tablespoons apricot mixture onto each rectangle. Sprinkle each with 1½ teaspoons sugar-cinnamon mixture and ¼ cup pistachios. Cut each dough rectangle in half lengthwise into two 12×5-inch pieces. Roll up each piece jelly-roll style, starting with long side.

5. Cut each roll into 16 slices. Place slices on prepared cookie sheets. Spray tops of cookies with cooking spray; sprinkle with remaining sugar-cinnamon mixture.

6. Bake 16 minutes or until golden. Cool cookies on cookie sheets 2 minutes. Remove to wire racks; cool completely. *Makes 64 cookies*

....

Nutrients per Serving (1 cookie): Calories: 45, Calories from Fat: 60%, Total Fat: 3g, Saturated Fat: <1g, Cholesterol: 3mg, Sodium: 34mg, Carbohydrate: 5g, Fiber: <1g, Protein: 1g

Pistachio Pinwheels

• Cookies, **Bars & Bites** •

PM Snack Bars

3 tablespoons creamy peanut butter
2 tablespoons molasses
2 egg whites
2 tablespoons ground flax seeds
4 cups crisp rice cereal
$^{1}/_{2}$ cup sliced almonds
1 ounce bittersweet chocolate, melted

1. Preheat oven to 350°F. Spray 9-inch square baking pan with nonstick cooking spray. Place peanut butter in small microwavable bowl; microwave on LOW (30%) 30 seconds or until peanut butter is melted. Stir in molasses; cool.

2. Place egg whites and flax seeds in blender; blend until foamy. Pour into large bowl. Add peanut butter mixture; stir until smooth. Stir in cereal and almonds until cereal is evenly coated. Press cereal mixture into prepared pan.

3. Bake 20 to 25 minutes or until lightly browned. Cool completely in pan on wire rack. Cut into bars. Drizzle melted chocolate over bars. *Makes 16 bars*

Tip: Look for ground flax seeds in large supermarkets or health food stores. You may also buy whole flax seeds and grind them in a coffee mill or blender.

Nutrients per Serving (1 bar): Calories: 91, Calories from Fat: 41%, Total Fat: 4g, Saturated Fat: 1g, Cholesterol: <1mg, Sodium: 24mg, Carbohydrate: 11g, Fiber: 1g, Protein: 3g

68 calories

• Cookies, **Bars & Bites** •

Tropical Sugar Cookie Bars

1 package (17$\frac{1}{2}$ ounces) sugar cookie mix
$\frac{1}{3}$ cup canola oil
1 egg
$\frac{1}{2}$ cup apricot fruit spread
1 teaspoon grated fresh ginger
1 can (8 ounces) pineapple tidbits, drained
1 mango, peeled, seeded and diced
1 medium kiwi, peeled and diced
2 cups fresh strawberries, stemmed and diced

1. Preheat oven to 350°F. Line bottom and sides of 13×9-inch baking pan with foil. Spray foil with nonstick cooking spray.

2. Stir cookie mix, oil and egg in medium bowl until well mixed. Spread dough evenly in prepared pan.

3. Bake 23 minutes or until golden. Gently lift cookie out of pan using foil. Cool completely on wire rack.

4. Place fruit spread in small microwavable bowl. Microwave on HIGH 1 minute or until slightly melted. Stir in ginger. Spread apricot mixture evenly over cookie. Arrange fruit over top. Cut into bars. *Makes 24 bars*

Nutrients per Serving (1 bar with 2 tablespoons fruit): Calories: 68, Calories from Fat: 53%, Total Fat: 4g, Saturated Fat: <1g, Cholesterol: 9mg, Sodium: 12mg, Carbohydrate: 9g, Fiber: 1g, Protein: 1g

Tropical Sugar Cookie Bars

• Cookies, **Bars & Bites** •

Oatmeal-Date Cookies

$^1/_2$ cup packed light brown sugar
$^1/_4$ cup ($^1/_2$ stick) margarine, softened
1 whole egg
1 egg white
1 tablespoon frozen apple juice concentrate
1 teaspoon vanilla
1$^1/_2$ cups all-purpose flour
2 teaspoons baking soda
$^1/_4$ teaspoon salt
1$^1/_2$ cups quick oats
$^1/_2$ cup chopped dates or raisins

1. Preheat oven to 350°F. Lightly spray cookie sheets with nonstick cooking spray.

2. Beat brown sugar and margarine in large bowl with electric mixer at medium speed until well blended. Add egg, egg white, apple juice concentrate and vanilla; beat until well blended.

3. Add flour, baking soda and salt; mix well. Stir in oats and dates. Drop dough by teaspoonfuls onto prepared cookie sheets.

4. Bake 8 to 10 minutes or until edges are very lightly browned. (Centers should still be soft.)

5. Cool cookies on cookie sheets 1 minute. Remove to wire racks; cool completely.

Makes 36 cookies

Nutrients per Serving (1 cookie): Calories: 65, Calories from Fat: 27%, Total Fat: 2g, Saturated Fat: <1g, Cholesterol: 6mg, Sodium: 106mg, Carbohydrate: 11g, Fiber: 1g, Protein: 1g

• Cookies, **Bars & Bites** •

Chocolate Cherry Cookies

1 package (9 ounces) chocolate cake mix
3 tablespoons fat-free (skim) milk
$1/2$ teaspoon almond extract
10 to 12 maraschino cherries, rinsed, drained and cut into halves
2 tablespoons white chocolate chips
$1/2$ teaspoon canola oil

1. Preheat oven to 350°F. Spray cookie sheets with nonstick cooking spray.

2. Beat cake mix, milk and almond extract in medium bowl with electric mixer at low speed. Increase speed to medium when mixture looks crumbly; beat 2 minutes or until smooth dough forms. (Dough will be very sticky.)

3. Coat hands with cooking spray. Shape dough into 1-inch balls. Place balls $2^1/2$ inches apart on prepared cookie sheets. Flatten each ball slightly. Place cherry half in center of each cookie.

4. Bake 8 to 9 minutes or until cookies are no longer shiny and tops begin to crack. Remove to wire racks; cool completely.

5. Place white chocolate chips and oil in small microwavable bowl. Microwave on HIGH 30 seconds; stir. Repeat as necessary until chips are melted and mixture is smooth. Drizzle white chocolate glaze over cookies. Let stand until set.

Makes about 24 cookies

Nutrients per Serving (1 cookie): Calories: 54, Calories from Fat: 17%, Total Fat: 1g, Saturated Fat: 1g, Cholesterol: <1mg, Sodium: 79mg, Carbohydrate: 10g, Fiber: <1g, Protein: 1g

Chocolate Cherry Cookies

·Tasty· Tidbits

Mediterranean Pita Pizzas

2 (8-inch) pita bread rounds
1 teaspoon olive oil
1 cup canned cannellini beans, rinsed and drained
2 teaspoons lemon juice
2 cloves garlic, minced
$\frac{1}{2}$ cup thinly sliced radicchio or escarole lettuce (optional)
$\frac{1}{2}$ cup chopped seeded tomato
$\frac{1}{2}$ cup finely chopped red onion
$\frac{1}{4}$ cup (1 ounce) crumbled feta cheese
2 tablespoons sliced pitted black olives

1. Preheat oven to 450°F. Arrange pitas on baking sheet; brush tops with oil. Bake 6 minutes.

2. Meanwhile, place beans in small bowl; mash lightly with fork. Stir in lemon juice and garlic.

3. Spread bean mixture evenly on pitas to within $\frac{1}{2}$ inch of edges. Top with radicchio, if desired, tomato, onion, feta and olives.

4. Bake 5 minutes or until toppings are thoroughly heated and crust is crisp. Cut into quarters; serve hot. *Makes 8 servings*

Nutrients per Serving (1 wedge): Calories: 98, Calories from Fat: 29%, Total Fat: 3g, Saturated Fat: 1g, Cholesterol: 7mg, Sodium: 282mg, Carbohydrate: 14g, Fiber: 2g, Protein: 4g

Stuffed Baguette

2 medium red bell peppers
1 loaf French bread (about 14 inches long)
¼ cup plus 2 tablespoons fat-free Italian dressing, divided
1 small red onion, very thinly sliced
8 large fresh basil leaves
3 ounces Swiss cheese, very thinly sliced

1. Preheat oven to 425°F. Line large baking sheet with foil.

2. To roast bell peppers, cut in half; remove stems, seeds and membranes. Place peppers, cut sides down, on prepared baking sheet. Bake 20 to 25 minutes or until skins are browned.

3. Transfer peppers to paper bag; close bag. Let stand 10 minutes or until peppers are cool enough to handle and skins are loosened. Peel off and discard skins; cut peppers into strips.

4. Trim ends from bread. Cut loaf in half lengthwise. Remove soft insides of loaf and reserve for another use.

5. Brush ¼ cup Italian dressing evenly onto cut sides of bread. Arrange pepper strips on bottom half of loaf; top with onion. Brush onion with remaining 2 tablespoons Italian dressing; top with basil and cheese. Replace top half of loaf. Wrap loaf tightly in plastic wrap; refrigerate at least 2 hours.

6. Cut loaf crosswise into 1-inch slices. Secure with toothpicks.

Makes 12 servings

Nutrients per Serving (1 slice): Calories: 98, Calories from Fat: 25%, Total Fat: 3g, Saturated Fat: 1g, Cholesterol: 7mg, Sodium: 239mg, Carbohydrate: 14g, Fiber: 1g, Protein: 4g

Stuffed Baguette

• Tasty **Tidbits** •

New Wave Chicken Salad Wraps

2 cups chopped fresh spinach
1¹/₂ cups chopped cooked chicken breast (about 8 ounces uncooked)
1 cup chopped fresh tomatoes
1 cup shredded carrots
1 cup frozen corn, thawed
2 teaspoons garlic-herb seasoning
¹/₄ cup reduced-fat mayonnaise
16 leaves romaine, iceberg or Bibb lettuce

1. Combine all ingredients except lettuce in large bowl; mix well.

2. To serve, spoon ¹/₄ cup chicken mixture onto each lettuce leaf; roll or fold as desired. *Makes 8 servings*

Nutrients per Serving (2 wraps): Calories: 93, Calories from Fat: 31%, Total Fat: 3g, Saturated Fat: <1g, Cholesterol: 23mg, Sodium: 98mg, Carbohydrate: 7g, Fiber: 2g, Protein: 9g

Mini Cheese Burritos

¹/₂ cup canned fat-free refried beans
4 (8-inch) fat-free flour tortillas
¹/₂ cup chunky salsa
4 (³/₄-ounce) reduced-fat Cheddar cheese sticks*

Reduced-fat Cheddar cheese block can be substituted. Cut cheese into sticks.

Microwave Directions

1. Spread beans over tortillas, leaving ¹/₂ inch border around edges. Spoon salsa over beans.

2. Place cheese stick on one side of each tortilla. Fold edge of tortilla over cheese stick; roll up. Place burritos, seam side down, in microwavable dish.

3. Microwave on HIGH 1 to 2 minutes or until cheese is melted. Let stand 1 to 2 minutes before serving. *Makes 4 servings*

Nutrients per Serving (1 burrito): Calories: 109, Calories from Fat: 31%, Total Fat: 4g, Saturated Fat: 3g, Cholesterol: 10mg, Sodium: 435mg, Carbohydrate: 11g, Fiber: 4g, Protein: 9g

New Wave Chicken Salad Wraps

Tomato-Herb Soup

1 can (about 14 ounces) no-salt-added diced tomatoes
1 can (about 14 ounces) reduced-sodium chicken broth
1 package (8 ounces) frozen bell pepper stir-fry mixture
1 cup frozen green beans
$\frac{1}{2}$ cup water
1 tablespoon ketchup
1 to 2 teaspoons dried oregano
1 teaspoon dried basil
$\frac{1}{8}$ teaspoon red pepper flakes (optional)
1 tablespoon olive oil
$\frac{1}{2}$ teaspoon salt (optional)

1. Combine tomatoes, broth, bell peppers, green beans, water, ketchup, oregano, basil and red pepper flakes, if desired, in large saucepan. Bring to a boil over high heat. Reduce heat; cover and simmer 20 minutes or until beans are tender.

2. Remove from heat. Stir in oil and salt, if desired.   *Makes 4 servings*

Variation: Substitute chopped fresh bell peppers for the frozen stir-fry mix.

Nutrients per Serving: Calories: 94, Calories from Fat: 28%, Total Fat: 3g, Saturated Fat: <1g, Cholesterol: 0mg, Sodium: 327mg, Carbohydrate: 14g, Fiber: 4g, Protein: 3g

Tomato-Herb Soup

• Tasty **Tidbits** •

Black Bean Quesadillas

Nonstick cooking spray
4 (8-inch) flour tortillas
3/4 cup (3 ounces) shredded reduced-fat Monterey Jack or Cheddar cheese
1/2 cup canned black beans, rinsed and drained
2 green onions, sliced
1/4 cup chopped fresh cilantro
1/2 teaspoon ground cumin
1/2 cup salsa
2 tablespoons plus 2 teaspoons fat-free sour cream
Additional fresh cilantro (optional)

1. Preheat oven to 450°F. Spray large nonstick baking sheet with cooking spray. Place two tortillas on prepared baking sheet; sprinkle each with half of cheese.

2. Combine beans, green onions, cilantro and cumin in small bowl; mix lightly. Spoon bean mixture evenly over cheese; top with remaining tortillas. Spray tops with cooking spray.

3. Bake 10 to 12 minutes or until cheese is melted and tortillas are lightly browned. Cut into quarters; top each tortilla wedge with 1 tablespoon salsa and 1 teaspoon sour cream. Garnish with cilantro. *Makes 8 servings*

Nutrients per Serving (1 wedge with 1 tablespoon salsa and 1 teaspoon sour cream): Calories: 105, Calories from Fat: 34%, Total Fat: 4g, Saturated Fat: 1g, Cholesterol: 8mg, Sodium: 259mg, Carbohydrate: 13g, Fiber: 1g, Protein: 7g

Tip The possibilities for quesadilla fillings are endless. Try veggies such as bell peppers, mushrooms, zucchini or squash. Any cheese would work well, even a nontraditional one like goat cheese. For heartier quesadillas, add chopped cooked chicken, beef or pork.

Black Bean Quesadilla

• Tasty **Tidbits** •

Peppered Shrimp Skewers

¹/₃ **cup teriyaki sauce**
¹/₃ **cup ketchup**
  2 **tablespoons dry sherry or water**
  2 **tablespoons reduced-fat peanut butter**
  1 **teaspoon hot pepper sauce**
¹/₄ **teaspoon ground ginger**
  2 **large yellow bell peppers**
32 **large raw shrimp (about 1¹/₂ pounds), peeled and deveined, with tails on**
32 **fresh sugar snap peas, trimmed**

1. Soak 16 (12-inch) wooden skewers in water at least 20 minutes before assembling kabobs.

2. Preheat broiler. Spray broiler pan with nonstick cooking spray.

3. Combine teriyaki sauce, ketchup, sherry, peanut butter, pepper sauce and ginger in small saucepan. Bring to a boil, stirring constantly. Reduce heat to low; simmer 1 minute. Remove from heat.

4. Cut each bell pepper lengthwise into four quarters; remove stems and seeds. Cut each quarter crosswise into four equal pieces. Thread two shrimp, two bell pepper pieces and two sugar snap peas onto each skewer; place on prepared pan. Brush with teriyaki sauce mixture.

5. Broil skewers 4 inches from heat 3 minutes; turn. Brush with teriyaki sauce mixture; broil 2 minutes or until shrimp turn pink and opaque. Discard any remaining teriyaki sauce mixture.   *Makes 16 servings*

Nutrients per Serving (1 skewer): Calories: 79, Calories from Fat: 23%, Total Fat: 2g, Saturated Fat: <1g, Cholesterol: 66mg, Sodium: 245mg, Carbohydrate: 7g, Fiber: 1g, Protein: 10g

Peppered Shrimp Skewer

• Tasty **Tidbits** •

Mini Chickpea Cakes

1 can (about 15 ounces) chickpeas, rinsed and drained
1 cup shredded carrots
¹⁄₃ cup seasoned dry bread crumbs
¹⁄₄ cup reduced-fat creamy Italian salad dressing, plus additional for dipping
1 egg

1. Preheat oven to 375°F. Spray baking sheets with nonstick cooking spray.

2. Coarsely mash chickpeas in medium bowl with potato masher. Stir in carrots, bread crumbs, ¹⁄₄ cup salad dressing and egg; mix well.

3. Shape chickpea mixture into 24 patties, using about 1 tablespoon mixture for each. Place on prepared baking sheets.

4. Bake 15 to 18 minutes or until chickpea cakes are lightly browned on both sides, turning halfway through baking time. Serve warm with additional salad dressing for dipping, if desired. *Makes 8 servings*

Nutrients per Serving (3 cakes without additional dressing): Calories: 102, Calories from Fat: 17%, Total Fat: 2g, Saturated Fat: 1g, Cholesterol: 27mg, Sodium: 314mg, Carbohydrate: 17g, Fiber: 3g, Protein: 4g

Crostini with Lemony Pesto

33 calories

1 (4-ounce) French baguette
3 tablespoons pesto
¹⁄₂ teaspoon lemon juice
¹⁄₂ cup chopped plum tomato

1. Preheat oven to 350°F.

2. Cut baguette crosswise into 16 slices; arrange on baking sheet. Bake 11 to 12 minutes or until bread begins to brown. Cool completely.

3. Combine pesto and lemon juice in small bowl; stir until well blended. Spread each bread slice with ¹⁄₂ teaspoon pesto mixture. Top with tomato. Serve immediately. *Makes 16 servings*

Nutrients per Serving (1 crostino): Calories: 33, Calories from Fat: 39%, Total Fat: 1g, Saturated Fat: <1g, Cholesterol: <1mg, Sodium: 64mg, Carbohydrate: 4g, Fiber: <1g, Protein: 1g

Mini Chickpea Cakes

• Tasty **Tidbits** •

Caribbean Chutney Kabobs

$^1/_2$ **medium pineapple**
$^3/_4$ **pound boneless skinless chicken breasts, cut into 1-inch pieces**
  1 medium red bell pepper, cut into 1-inch pieces
$^1/_2$ **cup mango chutney**
  2 tablespoons orange juice or pineapple juice
  1 teaspoon vanilla
$^1/_4$ **teaspoon ground nutmeg**

1. Soak 20 (4-inch) wooden skewers in water at least 20 minutes before assembling kabobs.

2. Peel and core pineapple. Cut pineapple into 1-inch chunks. Alternately thread chicken, pineapple and bell pepper onto skewers. Place in shallow baking dish.

3. Combine chutney, orange juice, vanilla and nutmeg in small bowl; mix well. Pour over kabobs. Cover and refrigerate up to 4 hours.

4. Preheat broiler. Spray broiler pan with nonstick cooking spray. Place kabobs on prepared pan; discard marinade.

5. Broil kabobs 6 to 8 inches from heat 4 to 5 minutes per side or until chicken is cooked through. *Makes 10 servings*

Nutrients per Serving (2 kabobs): Calories: 108, Calories from Fat: 10%, Total Fat: 1g, Saturated Fat: <1g, Cholesterol: 21mg, Sodium: 22mg, Carbohydrate: 16g, Fiber: 2g, Protein: 8g

Caribbean Chutney Kabobs

• Tasty **Tidbits** •

Veggie Pizza Pitas

2 whole wheat pita bread rounds, cut in half horizontally (to make 4 rounds)
¼ cup pizza sauce
1 teaspoon dried basil
⅛ teaspoon red pepper flakes (optional)
1 cup sliced mushrooms
½ cup thinly sliced green bell pepper
½ cup thinly sliced red onion
½ cup (2 ounces) shredded mozzarella cheese
2 teaspoons grated Parmesan cheese

1. Preheat oven to 475°F.

2. Arrange pitas, rough sides up, in single layer on large nonstick baking sheet. Spread 1 tablespoon pizza sauce evenly over each round to within ¼ inch of edge. Sprinkle with basil and red pepper flakes, if desired. Top with mushrooms, bell pepper and onion. Sprinkle with mozzarella.

3. Bake 5 minutes or until cheese is melted. Sprinkle ½ teaspoon Parmesan over each pizza. *Makes 4 servings*

Nutrients per Serving (1 pizza): Calories: 87, Calories from Fat: 21%, Total Fat: 2g, Saturated Fat: <1g, Cholesterol: 4mg, Sodium: 293mg, Carbohydrate: 12g, Fiber: 2g, Protein: 7g

Veggie Pizza Pita

Asian Vegetable Rolls with Soy-Lime Dipping Sauce

¹⁄₄ cup reduced-sodium soy sauce
 2 tablespoons lime juice
 1 clove garlic, crushed
 1 teaspoon honey
¹⁄₂ teaspoon finely chopped fresh ginger
¹⁄₄ teaspoon dark sesame oil
¹⁄₈ to ¹⁄₄ teaspoon red pepper flakes
¹⁄₂ cup grated cucumber
¹⁄₃ cup grated carrot
¹⁄₄ cup sliced yellow bell pepper (1 inch long)
 2 tablespoons thinly sliced green onion
 18 small lettuce leaves
     Sesame seeds (optional)

1. Combine soy sauce, lime juice, garlic, honey, ginger, oil and red pepper flakes in small bowl.

2. Combine cucumber, carrot, bell pepper and green onion in medium bowl. Stir in 1 tablespoon soy sauce mixture.

3. Place about 1 tablespoon vegetable mixture on each lettuce leaf. Roll up leaves; sprinkle with sesame seeds, if desired. Serve with remaining sauce for dipping.

Makes 6 servings

Nutrients per Serving (3 rolls with 1 tablespoon dipping sauce): Calories: 25, Calories from Fat: 11%, Total Fat: <1g, Saturated Fat: <1g, Cholesterol: 0mg, Sodium: 343mg, Carbohydrate: 5g, Fiber: 1g, Protein: 1g

Open-Faced Egg Salad Sandwiches

6 hard-cooked eggs
3 tablespoons reduced-fat mayonnaise
$\frac{1}{2}$ cup finely chopped green onions
1$\frac{1}{2}$ tablespoons sweet pickle relish
$\frac{1}{4}$ to $\frac{1}{2}$ teaspoon celery seed
$\frac{1}{4}$ teaspoon salt
$\frac{1}{8}$ teaspoon black pepper
4 slices reduced-calorie, high-fiber bread
2 cups packed spring greens

1. Separate egg yolks from whites; discard 4 yolks or reserve for another use.

2. Combine remaining 2 egg yolks and mayonnaise in medium bowl; mix well. Finely chop egg whites and add to mixture. Stir in green onions, pickle relish, celery seed, salt and pepper; mix well.

3. Top each bread slice evenly with greens and egg salad.   *Makes 4 servings*

Nutrients per Serving: Calories: 104, Calories from Fat: 23%, Total Fat: 3g, Saturated Fat: <1g, Cholesterol: 104mg, Sodium: 400mg, Carbohydrate: 14g, Fiber: 6g, Protein: 9g

To prepare hard-cooked eggs, place the eggs in a single layer in a saucepan. Add cold water to cover the eggs by 1 inch; cover and bring to a boil over high heat. Remove the pan from the heat and let stand 15 minutes. Immediately pour off the water, cover the eggs with cold water and let stand until the eggs have cooled.

Open-Faced Egg Salad Sandwich

• Tasty **Tidbits** •

Wild Wedges

2 (8-inch) fat-free flour tortillas
Nonstick cooking spray
1/3 cup shredded reduced-fat Cheddar cheese
1/3 cup chopped cooked chicken or turkey
1 green onion, thinly sliced
2 tablespoons mild thick and chunky salsa

1. Heat large nonstick skillet over medium heat.

2. Spray one side of one tortilla with cooking spray; place in skillet sprayed side down. Top with cheese, chicken, green onion and salsa. Top with remaining tortilla; spray with cooking spray.

3. Cook 2 to 3 minutes per side or until golden brown and cheese is melted. Cut into 8 wedges. *Makes 4 servings*

Variation: For bean quesadillas, omit the chicken and spread 1/3 cup canned fat-free refried beans over one of the tortillas.

. . . .

Nutrients per Serving (2 wedges): Calories: 82, Calories from Fat: 25%, Total Fat: 2g, Saturated Fat: 1g, Cholesterol: 13mg, Sodium: 224mg, Carbohydrate: 8g, Fiber: 3g, Protein: 7g

Rotisserie chicken is one of the most popular convenience products at the supermarket—with good reason. One whole cooked chicken will yield about 2 1/2 cups chopped chicken, enough to use in several snacks or meals throughout the week.

Angelic Deviled Eggs

6 eggs
¼ cup low-fat (1%) cottage cheese
3 tablespoons fat-free ranch dressing
2 teaspoons Dijon mustard
2 tablespoons minced fresh chives or dill
1 tablespoon diced well-drained pimiento or roasted red pepper

1. Place eggs in medium saucepan; add enough water to cover by 1 inch. Cover and bring to a boil over high heat. Remove from heat; let stand 15 minutes. Drain. Add cold water to eggs in saucepan; let stand until eggs are cool. Drain and peel.

2. Cut eggs in half lengthwise. Remove yolks, reserving 3 yolk halves. Discard remaining yolks or reserve for another use. Place egg whites, cut sides up, on serving plate; cover with plastic wrap. Refrigerate while preparing filling.

3. Combine cottage cheese, dressing, mustard and reserved yolk halves in small bowl; mash with fork until well blended. Stir in chives and pimiento. Spoon into egg whites. Cover and refrigerate at least 1 hour. *Makes 12 servings*

Nutrients per Serving (1 egg half): Calories: 44, Calories from Fat: 52%, Total Fat: 3g, Saturated Fat: <1g, Cholesterol: 27mg, Sodium: 96mg, Carbohydrate: 1g, Fiber: 1g, Protein: 4g

· Munchies ·
& Things

Savory Zucchini Sticks

   Nonstick cooking spray
3 tablespoons seasoned dry bread crumbs
2 tablespoons grated Parmesan cheese
1 egg white
1 teaspoon reduced-fat (2%) milk
2 small zucchini (about 4 ounces each), cut lengthwise into quarters
¹⁄₃ cup pasta sauce, warmed

1. Preheat oven to 400°F. Spray baking sheet with cooking spray.

2. Combine bread crumbs and Parmesan in shallow dish. Combine egg white and milk in another shallow dish; beat with fork until well blended.

3. Dip each zucchini stick first into crumb mixture, then into egg white mixture, letting excess drip back into dish. Roll again in crumb mixture to coat. Place zucchini sticks on prepared baking sheet; spray with cooking spray.

4. Bake 15 to 18 minutes or until golden brown. Serve with pasta sauce.

Makes 4 servings

Nutrients per Serving (2 sticks with 4 teaspoons pasta sauce): Calories: 69, Calories from Fat: 26%, Total Fat: 2g, Saturated Fat: 1g, Cholesterol: 6mg, Sodium: 329mg, Carbohydrate: 9g, Fiber: 1g, Protein: 4g

•Munchies & Things•

Taco Popcorn Olé

9 cups air-popped popcorn
Butter-flavored cooking spray
1 teaspoon chili powder
¹/₂ teaspoon salt
¹/₂ teaspoon garlic powder
¹/₈ teaspoon ground red pepper (optional)

1. Preheat oven to 350°F. Line 15×10×1-inch jelly-roll pan with foil.

2. Place popcorn in single layer on prepared pan. Spray lightly with cooking spray.

3. Combine chili powder, salt, garlic powder and red pepper, if desired, in small bowl. Sprinkle spice mixture over popcorn; mix lightly to coat.

4. Bake 5 minutes or until heated through, stirring gently after 3 minutes. Spread popcorn in single layer on large sheet of foil to cool.   *Makes 6 servings*

Tip: Store popcorn in tightly covered container at room temperature up to 4 days.

Nutrients per Serving (1¹/₂ cups): Calories: 48, Calories from Fat: 18%, Total Fat: 1g, Saturated Fat: <1g, Cholesterol: 0mg, Sodium: 199mg, Carbohydrate: 10g, Fiber: 2g, Protein: 2g

 For a spicier version, substitute a hot Mexican-style chili powder or a chipotle chili powder for the regular chili powder, or add the ground red pepper.

•Munchies **& Things**•

Spiced Sesame Wonton Crisps

20 (3-inch) wonton wrappers, cut in half
 1 tablespoon water
 2 teaspoons olive oil
$\frac{1}{2}$ teaspoon paprika
$\frac{1}{2}$ teaspoon ground cumin or chili powder
$\frac{1}{4}$ teaspoon dry mustard
 1 tablespoon sesame seeds

1. Preheat oven to 375°F. Spray baking sheets with nonstick cooking spray.

2. Cut each halved wonton wrapper into 2 strips; place in single layer on prepared baking sheets.

3. Combine water, oil, paprika, cumin and mustard in small bowl; mix well. Brush oil mixture evenly onto wonton strips; sprinkle with sesame seeds.

4. Bake 6 to 8 minutes or until lightly browned. Remove to wire racks; cool completely. *Makes 8 servings*

Nutrients per Serving (10 crisps): Calories: 75, Calories from Fat: 24%, Total Fat: 2g, Saturated Fat: <1g, Cholesterol: 3mg, Sodium: 116mg, Carbohydrate: 12g, Fiber: <1g, Protein: 2g

Creamy Dill Cheese Spread

 2 tablespoons reduced-fat cream cheese with herbs and garlic
 1 tablespoon reduced-fat mayonnaise
 1 tablespoon reduced-fat sour cream
 1 to 2 teaspoons chopped fresh dill
$\frac{1}{8}$ teaspoon salt (optional)
24 garlic-flavored melba rounds

1. Combine cream cheese, mayonnaise, sour cream, dill and salt, if desired, in small bowl. Cover with plastic wrap; refrigerate 1 hour.

2. To serve, top each melba round with $\frac{1}{2}$ teaspoon spread. *Makes 4 servings*

Nutrients per Serving (6 topped rounds): Calories: 95, Calories from Fat: 28%, Total Fat: 3g, Saturated Fat: 1g, Cholesterol: 6mg, Sodium: 170mg, Carbohydrate: 14g, Fiber: 1g, Protein: 2g

Spiced Sesame Wonton Crisps

• Munchies & Things •

Herbed Potato Chips

Nonstick cooking spray
2 unpeeled medium red potatoes (about ¹/₂ pound), very thinly sliced
1 tablespoon olive oil
2 tablespoons minced fresh dill, thyme or rosemary leaves *or* 2 teaspoons dried dill weed, thyme or rosemary
¹/₄ teaspoon garlic salt
¹/₈ teaspoon black pepper
1¹/₄ cups fat-free sour cream

1. Preheat oven to 450°F. Spray baking sheets with cooking spray. Pat potatoes dry with paper towels. Arrange in single layer on prepared baking sheets; spray with cooking spray.

2. Bake 10 minutes; turn slices. Brush with oil. Combine dill, garlic salt and pepper in small bowl; sprinkle evenly on potatoes. Bake 5 to 10 minutes or until golden brown. Cool on baking sheets. Serve with sour cream. *Makes 6 servings*

Nutrients per Serving (10 chips with about 3 tablespoons sour cream): Calories: 106, Calories from Fat: 17%, Total Fat: 2g, Saturated Fat: <1g, Cholesterol: 8mg, Sodium: 84mg, Carbohydrate: 16g, Fiber: 1g, Protein: 4g

Rosemary-Scented Nut Mix

108 calories

2 tablespoons unsalted butter
2 cups pecan halves
1 cup unsalted macadamia nuts
1 cup walnuts
1 teaspoon dried rosemary
¹/₂ teaspoon salt
¹/₄ teaspoon red pepper flakes

1. Preheat oven to 300°F. Melt butter in large saucepan over low heat. Add pecans, macadamia nuts and walnuts; mix well. Add rosemary, salt and red pepper flakes; cook and stir about 1 minute.

2. Spread mixture onto ungreased nonstick baking sheet. Bake 15 minutes, stirring occasionally. Cool completely on baking sheet on wire rack. *Makes 32 servings*

Nutrients per Serving (2 tablespoons): Calories: 108, Calories from Fat: 92%, Total Fat: 11g, Saturated Fat: 2g, Cholesterol: 2mg, Sodium: 37mg, Carbohydrate: 2g, Fiber: 1g, Protein: 2g

Herbed Potato Chips

• Munchies **& Things** •

Southwest Snack Mix

4 cups unsweetened corn cereal squares
2 cups unsalted pretzels
1/2 cup unsalted pumpkin or squash seeds
1 1/2 teaspoons chili powder
1 teaspoon minced fresh cilantro or parsley
1/2 teaspoon garlic powder
1/2 teaspoon onion powder
1 egg white
2 tablespoons olive oil
2 tablespoons lime juice

1. Preheat oven to 300°F. Spray baking sheet with nonstick cooking spray.

2. Combine cereal, pretzels and pumpkin seeds in large bowl. Combine chili powder, cilantro, garlic powder and onion powder in small bowl.

3. Whisk egg white, oil and lime juice in separate small bowl until well blended. Pour over cereal mixture; toss to coat. Add seasoning mixture; mix lightly to coat. Transfer to prepared baking sheet.

4. Bake 45 minutes, stirring every 15 minutes. Cool completely. Store in airtight container. *Makes about 12 servings*

Variation: Substitute 1/2 cup unsalted peanuts for pumpkin seeds.

Nutrients per Serving (1/2 cup): Calories: 93, Calories from Fat: 28%, Total Fat: 3g, Saturated Fat: <1g, Cholesterol: 0mg, Sodium: 114mg, Carbohydrate: 15g, Fiber: 1g, Protein: 2g

Southwest Snack Mix

● Munchies & Things ●

Great Zukes Pizza Bites

1 medium zucchini
3 tablespoons pizza sauce
2 tablespoons tomato paste
¼ teaspoon dried oregano
¾ cup (3 ounces) shredded mozzarella cheese
¼ cup shredded Parmesan cheese
8 slices pitted black olives
8 slices pepperoni

1. Preheat broiler; set rack 4 inches from heat.

2. Trim off and discard ends of zucchini. Cut zucchini into 16 (¼-inch-thick) diagonal slices. Place on nonstick baking sheet.

3. Combine pizza sauce, tomato paste and oregano in small bowl; mix well. Spread scant teaspoon sauce over each zucchini slice. Combine cheeses in small bowl. Top each zucchini slice with 1 tablespoon cheese mixture, pressing down into sauce. Place one olive slice on each of eight pizza bites. Place one folded pepperoni slice on each remaining pizza bite.

4. Broil 3 minutes or until cheese is melted. Serve immediately.   *Makes 8 servings*

Nutrients per Serving (2 bites): Calories: 75, Calories from Fat: 60%, Total Fat: 5g, Saturated Fat: 2g, Cholesterol: 10mg, Sodium: 288mg, Carbohydrate: 3g, Fiber: 1g, Protein: 5g

Great Zukes Pizza Bites

• Munchies **& Things** •

Peppy Snack Mix

3 (3-inch) plain rice cakes, broken into bite-size pieces
1¹/₂ cups bite-size frosted shredded wheat cereal
³/₄ cup pretzel sticks, halved
3 tablespoons reduced-fat margarine, melted
2 teaspoons reduced-sodium Worcestershire sauce
³/₄ teaspoon chili powder
¹/₈ to ¹/₄ teaspoon ground red pepper

1. Preheat oven to 300°F. Combine rice cake pieces, cereal and pretzels in 13×9-inch baking pan.

2. Combine margarine, Worcestershire sauce, chili powder and red pepper in small bowl. Drizzle over cereal mixture; toss to combine.

3. Bake 20 minutes, stirring after 10 minutes. *Makes 8 servings*

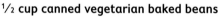

Nutrients per Serving (¹/₂ cup): Calories: 94, Calories from Fat: 23%, Total Fat: 2g, Saturated Fat: <1g, Cholesterol: 0mg, Sodium: 125mg, Carbohydrate: 16g, Fiber: <1g, Protein: 2g

Cheesy Barbecued Bean Dip

93
calories

¹/₂ cup canned vegetarian baked beans
3 tablespoons pasteurized process cheese product
2 tablespoons regular or hickory smoke barbecue sauce
2 large carrots, cut into diagonal slices
1 medium red or green bell pepper, cut into slices

Microwave Directions

1. Place beans in small microwavable bowl; mash slightly with fork. Stir in process cheese product and barbecue sauce. Cover with vented plastic wrap.

2. Microwave on HIGH 1 minute; stir. Microwave 30 seconds or until hot. Serve with carrot and bell pepper slices. *Makes 4 servings*

Nutrients per Serving: Calories: 93, Calories from Fat: 25%, Total Fat: 3g, Saturated Fat: 1g, Cholesterol: 10mg, Sodium: 355mg, Carbohydrate: 15g, Fiber: 4g, Protein: 4g

Peppy Snack Mix

Munchies & Things

Super Nachos

12 large baked reduced-fat tortilla chips (about 1$\frac{1}{2}$ ounces)
$\frac{1}{2}$ cup (2 ounces) shredded reduced-fat Cheddar cheese
$\frac{1}{4}$ cup fat-free refried beans
2 tablespoons chunky salsa
Fresh cilantro (optional)

Microwave Directions

1. Arrange chips in single layer on large microwavable plate. Sprinkle cheese evenly over chips.

2. Spoon 1 teaspoon beans over each chip; top with $\frac{1}{2}$ teaspoon salsa.

3. Microwave on MEDIUM (50%) 2 to 3 minutes or until cheese is melted. Garnish with cilantro.   *Makes 4 servings*

Conventional Directions: Preheat oven to 350°F. Line baking sheet with foil. Assemble nachos on prepared baking sheet as directed above. Bake 10 to 12 minutes or until cheese is melted.

Tip: For a single serving of nachos, arrange 3 large tortilla chips on a microwavable plate. Top chips with 2 tablespoons cheese, 1 tablespoon refried beans and about $\frac{1}{2}$ tablespoon salsa. Microwave on MEDIUM (50%) 1 to 1$\frac{1}{2}$ minutes or until cheese is melted.

Nutrients per Serving (3 nachos): Calories: 82, Calories from Fat: 44%, Total Fat: 4g, Saturated Fat: 2g, Cholesterol: 10mg, Sodium: 263mg, Carbohydrate: 6g, Fiber: 1g, Protein: 4g

Super Nachos

• Munchies & Things •

Savory Pita Chips

2 rounds whole wheat pita bread
Olive oil cooking spray
3 tablespoons grated Parmesan cheese
1 teaspoon dried basil
¼ teaspoon garlic powder

1. Preheat oven to 350°F. Line baking sheet with foil.

2. Cut each pita in half horizontally to make two rounds. Cut each round into six wedges.

3. Place wedges, rough side down, on prepared baking sheet; spray lightly with cooking spray. Turn wedges; spray again.

4. Combine Parmesan, basil and garlic powder in small bowl; sprinkle evenly over pita wedges.

5. Bake 12 to 14 minutes or until golden brown. Cool completely.

Makes 4 servings

Cinnamon Crisps: Substitute butter-flavored cooking spray for olive oil-flavored cooking spray, and 1 tablespoon sugar mixed with ¼ teaspoon ground cinnamon for Parmesan cheese, basil and garlic powder.

Nutrients per Serving (6 chips): Calories: 108, Calories from Fat: 18%, Total Fat: 2g, Saturated Fat: 1g, Cholesterol: 4mg, Sodium: 257mg, Carbohydrate: 18g, Fiber: 2g, Protein: 5g

• Munchies & Things •

BLT Cukes

½ cup finely chopped lettuce
½ cup finely chopped baby spinach
  3 slices bacon, crisp-cooked and crumbled
¼ cup finely diced tomato
  1 tablespoon plus 1½ teaspoons fat-free mayonnaise
¼ teaspoon black pepper
⅛ teaspoon salt
  1 large cucumber
    Minced fresh parsley or green onion (optional)

1. Combine lettuce, spinach, bacon, tomato, mayonnaise, pepper and salt in medium bowl; mix well.

2. Peel cucumber; trim off ends and cut in half lengthwise. Use spoon to scoop out seeds; discard seeds.

3. Divide bacon mixture between cucumber halves, mounding in center. Garnish with parsley. Cut into 2-inch pieces. *Makes 10 servings*

Tip: Make these snacks when cucumbers are plentiful and large enough to easily hollow out with a spoon. These snacks can be made, covered and refrigerated up to 12 hours ahead of time.

Nutrients per Serving (1 piece): Calories: 26, Calories from Fat: 69%, Total Fat: 2g, Saturated Fat: <1g, Cholesterol: 3mg, Sodium: 72mg, Carbohydrate: 2g, Fiber: <1g, Protein: 2g

·Frozen·
Pops

Banana & Chocolate Chip Pops

1 small ripe banana, sliced
1 cup banana nonfat yogurt
1/8 teaspoon ground nutmeg
2 tablespoons mini chocolate chips
Pop molds

1. Combine banana, yogurt and nutmeg in blender or food processor; blend until smooth. Stir in chocolate chips.

2. Spoon banana mixture into four plastic pop molds. Cover with lids. Freeze 2 hours or until firm.

3. To remove pops from molds, place bottoms of pops under warm running water until loosened. Press firmly on bottoms to release. (Do not twist or pull sticks.)

Makes 4 pops

Peanut Butter & Jelly Pops: Stir 1/4 cup reduced-fat peanut butter in small bowl until smooth; stir in 1 cup vanilla nonfat yogurt. Drop 2 tablespoons strawberry fruit spread on top of mixture; pull spoon back and forth through mixture several times to swirl slightly. Spoon into four molds and freeze as directed above. Makes 4 servings.

Blueberry-Lime Pops: Stir 1 cup Key lime nonfat yogurt in small bowl until smooth; fold in 1/3 cup frozen blueberries. Spoon into four molds and freeze as directed above. Makes 4 servings.

Nutrients per Serving (1 pop): Calories: 103, Calories from Fat: 14%, Total Fat: 2g, Saturated Fat: <1g, Cholesterol: 1mg, Sodium: 37mg, Carbohydrate: 20g, Fiber: <1g, Protein: 3g

• Frozen **Pops** •

Double Melon Pops

2 cups cubed honeydew
4 teaspoons lime juice, divided
   Pop molds
2 cups cubed cantaloupe

1. Combine honeydew and 2 teaspoons lime juice in blender or food processor; blend until smooth.

2. Spoon about ¼ cup honeydew mixture evenly into pop molds. Cover with lids. Freeze 1 hour.

3. Combine cantaloupe and remaining 2 teaspoons lime juice in blender or food processor; blend until smooth.

4. Spoon evenly over cantaloupe mixture in pop molds. Cover with lids. Freeze 2 hours or until firm.

5. To remove pops from molds, place bottoms of pops under warm running water until loosened. Press firmly on bottoms to release. (Do not twist or pull sticks.)

Makes 5 pops

Nutrients per Serving (1 pop): Calories: 48, Calories from Fat: 0%, Total Fat: 0g, Saturated Fat: 0g, Cholesterol: 0mg, Sodium: 23mg, Carbohydrate: 12g, Fiber: 1g, Protein: 1g

Tip To make this recipe even easier, purchase cut-up melon from the salad bar or produce section of the supermarket.

50 calories

Frozen **Pops**

Peachy Pops

1 package (16 ounces) frozen sliced peaches, partially thawed
2 containers (6 ounces each) peach or vanilla nonfat yogurt
¹/₄ cup honey
12 (3-ounce) paper cups
12 wooden sticks
Colored sugar or sugar sprinkles (optional)

1. Combine peaches, yogurt and honey in blender or food processor; blend until smooth.

2. Pour mixture into cups. Cover each cup with small piece of foil. Freeze 1 hour.

3. Insert wooden sticks through center of foil. Freeze 3 hours or until firm.

4. Remove foil and peel away paper cups; roll pops in sugar, if desired. Serve immediately. *Makes 12 pops*

Nutrients per Serving (1 pop): Calories: 50, Calories from Fat: 0%, Total Fat: 0g, Saturated Fat: 0g, Cholesterol: 0mg, Sodium: 20mg, Carbohydrate: 13g, Fiber: 1g, Protein: 2g

Frozen Fudge Pops

92 calories

¹/₂ cup nonfat sweetened condensed milk
¹/₄ cup unsweetened cocoa powder
1¹/₄ cups evaporated skimmed milk
1 teaspoon vanilla
8 (5-ounce) paper or plastic cups
8 wooden sticks

1. Beat sweetened condensed milk and cocoa in medium bowl until blended. Add evaporated milk and vanilla; beat until smooth.

2. Pour mixture into cups. Cover each cup with small piece of foil. Freeze 2 hours.

3. Insert wooden sticks through center of foil. Freeze 4 hours or until firm.

4. To serve, remove foil and peel away paper cups or gently twist frozen pops out of plastic cups. *Makes 8 pops*

Nutrients per Serving (1 pop): Calories: 92, Calories from Fat: 1%, Total Fat: <1g, Saturated Fat: <1g, Cholesterol: 2mg, Sodium: 70mg, Carbohydrate: 17g, Fiber: 0g, Protein: 5g

Peachy Pops

• Frozen **Pops** •

Magic Rainbow Pops

1 envelope (¹/₄ ounce) unflavored gelatin
¹/₄ cup cold water
¹/₂ cup boiling water
1 container (6 ounces) raspberry or strawberry nonfat yogurt
Pop molds
1 container (6 ounces) lemon or orange nonfat yogurt
1 can (8¹/₄ ounces) apricots or peaches with juice

1. Combine gelatin and cold water in 2-cup glass measuring cup. Let stand 5 minutes to soften. Add boiling water. Stir until gelatin is completely dissolved. Cool to room temperature.

2. Combine raspberry yogurt and ¹/₄ cup gelatin mixture in small bowl; stir until completely blended. Fill each pop mold about one third full with raspberry mixture.* Freeze 30 to 60 minutes or until set.

3. Combine lemon yogurt and ¹/₄ cup gelatin mixture in small bowl; stir until completely blended. Evenly pour lemon mixture over raspberry layer in molds.* Freeze 30 to 60 minutes or until set.

4. Place apricots with juice and remaining ¹/₄ cup gelatin mixture in blender or food processor; blend until smooth. Evenly pour apricot mixture into molds.* Cover with lids. Freeze 2 to 5 hours or until firm.

5. To remove pops from molds, place bottoms of pops under warm running water until loosened. Press firmly on bottoms to release. (Do not twist or pull sticks.)

Makes about 6 pops

Pour any extra mixture into small paper cups. Freeze as directed in the tip.

Nutrients per Serving (1 pop): Calories: 50, Calories from Fat: 0%, Total Fat: 0g, Saturated Fat: 0g, Cholesterol: 0mg, Sodium: 35mg, Carbohydrate: 11g, Fiber: 1g, Protein: 3g

 Tip

Three-ounce paper cups can be used in place of the molds. Make the layers as directed or put a single flavor in each cup. Freeze cups about 1 hour, then insert a wooden stick into the center of each cup. Freeze until firm.

• Frozen **Pops** •

Cherry-Peach Pops

¹/₃ cup peach or apricot nectar
1 teaspoon unflavored gelatin
1 can (15 ounces) sliced peaches in light syrup, drained
1 container (6 ounces) peach nonfat yogurt
1 container (6 ounces) cherry nonfat yogurt
7 (3-ounce) paper or plastic cups
7 wooden sticks

1. Combine nectar and gelatin in small saucepan; let stand 5 minutes. Cook over low heat just until gelatin dissolves, stirring occasionally.

2. Combine nectar mixture, drained peaches and yogurts in blender or food processor; blend until smooth.

3. Pour mixture into cups. Cover top of each cup with small piece of foil. Freeze 1 hour.

4. Insert wooden sticks through center of foil. Freeze 3 hours or until firm.

5. To serve, remove foil and peel away paper cups or gently twist frozen pops out of plastic cups. *Makes 7 pops*

Nutrients per Serving (1 pop): Calories: 80, Calories from Fat: 0%, Total Fat: 0g, Saturated Fat: 0g, Cholesterol: 0mg, Sodium: 35mg, Carbohydrate: 17g, Fiber: 0g, Protein: 3g

Cherry-Peach Pops

• Frozen **Pops** •

Candy Corn Pops

¼ cup vanilla ice cream
  Pop molds
1 cup mango, orange or peach sorbet
6 bamboo skewers
1 cup lemon sorbet
  Yellow food coloring

1. Place ice cream in small microwavable bowl; microwave on LOW (30%) 10 seconds. Whisk and microwave at 10-second intervals until ice cream reaches pourable consistency (about 5 times). Pour into pop molds, filling about one-third full. Freeze 30 minutes or until set.

2. Place mango sorbet in small microwavable bowl; microwave on LOW (30%) 10 seconds. Whisk and microwave at 10-second intervals until sorbet reaches pourable consistency (about 5 times). Pour into pop molds, filling about two-thirds full. Freeze 30 minutes or until set.

3. Insert skewers into each mold; freeze 1 hour or until firm.

4. Place lemon sorbet in small microwavable bowl; microwave on LOW (30%) 10 seconds. Whisk and microwave at 10-second intervals until sorbet reaches pourable consistency (about 5 times). Add yellow food coloring, a few drops at a time, until desired shade is reached. Pour into molds over sorbet. Freeze 5 hours or until firm.

5. To remove pops from molds, place bottoms of pops under warm running water until loosened. Press firmly on bottoms to release. (Do not twist or pull sticks.)

Makes 6 pops

Nutrients per Serving (1 pop): Calories: 90, Calories from Fat: 5%, Total Fat: <1g, Saturated Fat: 0g, Cholesterol: 0mg, Sodium: 15mg, Carbohydrate: 23g, Fiber: 0g, Protein: 0g

Candy Corn Pops

•Frozen **Pops**•

Creamy Strawberry-Orange Pops

1 cup strawberry nonfat yogurt
³/₄ cup orange juice
2 teaspoons vanilla
2 cups frozen whole strawberries
1 packet sugar substitute _or_ equivalent of 2 teaspoons sugar
6 (7-ounce) paper cups
6 wooden sticks

1. Combine yogurt, orange juice and vanilla in blender or food processor; blend until smooth. Add strawberries and sugar substitute; blend until smooth.

2. Pour mixture into cups. Cover each cup with small piece of foil. Freeze 1 hour.

3. Insert wooden sticks through center of foil. Freeze 4 hours or until firm.

4. To serve, remove foil and peel away paper cups or gently twist frozen pops out of plastic cups. _Makes 6 pops_

Nutrients per Serving (1 pop): Calories: 110, Calories from Fat: 0%, Total Fat: 0g, Saturated Fat: 0g, Cholesterol: 0mg, Sodium: 25mg, Carbohydrate: 26g, Fiber: 2g, Protein: 2g

 To make these pops even lighter in calories, use reduced-calorie orange juice or orange-flavored beverage instead of regular orange juice.

Creamy Strawberry-Orange Pops

• Frozen **Pops** •

Banana Freezer Pops

2 ripe medium bananas, sliced
1 can (6 ounces) frozen orange juice concentrate
¹⁄₄ cup water
1 tablespoon honey
1 teaspoon vanilla
8 (3-ounce) paper or plastic cups
8 wooden sticks

1. Combine bananas, orange juice concentrate, water, honey and vanilla in blender or food processor; blend until smooth.

2. Pour mixture into cups. Cover top of each cup with small piece of foil. Freeze 1 hour.

3. Insert wooden stick through center of foil into banana mixture. Freeze 3 hours or until firm.

4. To serve, remove foil and peel away paper cups or gently twist frozen pops out of plastic cups.
Makes 8 pops

Peppy Purple Pops: Omit honey and vanilla. Substitute grape juice concentrate for the orange juice concentrate.

Nutrients per Serving (1 pop): Calories: 83, Calories from Fat: 3%, Total Fat: <1g, Saturated Fat: <1g, Cholesterol: 0mg, Sodium: 1mg, Carbohydrate: 20g, Fiber: 1g, Protein: 1g

Banana Freezer Pops

·Smoothies·
& More

Frozen Watermelon Whip

1³/₄ cups ice
1 cup coarsely chopped seedless watermelon
1 cup brewed lemon-flavored herbal tea, cooled to room temperature
Lime slices (optional)

1. Combine ice, watermelon and tea in blender or food processor; blend until smooth, pulsing to break up ice.

2. Pour into two tall glasses. Garnish with lime. Serve immediately.

Makes 2 servings

Nutrients per Serving (1 smoothie): Calories: 24, Calories from Fat: 4%, Total Fat: <1g, Saturated Fat: <1g, Cholesterol: 0mg, Sodium: 2mg, Carbohydrate: 6g, Fiber: <1g, Protein: <1g

• Smoothies & More •

Berry Frost

1¹/₂ **cups ice**
1 **cup brewed raspberry-flavored herbal tea, cooled to room temperature**
1 **cup water**
¹/₂ **cup frozen unsweetened blueberries**
1 **tablespoon lime juice**
¹/₂ **teaspoon grated lime peel**

1. Combine all ingredients in blender or food processor; blend until smooth, pulsing to break up ice.

2. Pour into two tall glasses. Serve immediately. *Makes 2 servings*

Nutrients per Serving (1 smoothie): Calories: 23, Calories from Fat: 0%, Total Fat: <1g, Saturated Fat: <1g, Cholesterol: 0mg, Sodium: 2mg, Carbohydrate: 6g, Fiber: 1g, Protein: <1g

Wake-Me-Up Breakfast Smoothie

110
calories

2 **containers (6 ounces each) vanilla nonfat yogurt**
2 **cups sliced fresh strawberries**
1¹/₂ **cups ice**
1 **banana**
¹/₂ **cup fat-free (skim) milk**
2 **tablespoons wheat germ**
1 **tablespoon maple syrup**

1. Combine yogurt, strawberries, ice, banana, milk, wheat germ and maple syrup in blender or food processor; blend until smooth, stopping once to scrape down sides.

2. Pour into six glasses. Serve immediately. *Makes 6 servings*

Nutrients per Serving (1 smoothie): Calories: 110, Calories from Fat: 0%, Total Fat: 0g, Saturated Fat: 0g, Cholesterol: 0mg, Sodium: 55mg, Carbohydrate: 24g, Fiber: 2g, Protein: 5g

Berry Frost

•Smoothies **& More**•

Peachy Razz Refresher

1 cup ice
1 cup frozen sliced peaches
½ cup frozen raspberries
½ cup plain nonfat yogurt
½ cup orange juice
  Fresh peach slices (optional)
  Fresh raspberries (optional)

1. Combine ice, peaches, raspberries, yogurt and orange juice in blender or food processor; blend until smooth.

2. Pour into two glasses. Garnish with peach slices and fresh raspberries. Serve immediately. *Makes 2 servings*

Nutrients per Serving (1 smoothie): Calories: 100, Calories from Fat: 0%, Total Fat: 0g, Saturated Fat: 0g, Cholesterol: 0mg, Sodium: 50mg, Carbohydrate: 22g, Fiber: 2g, Protein: 5g

 For extra flavor, use peach or raspberry nonfat yogurt instead of plain yogurt.

Peachy Razz Refresher

• Smoothies & More •

Strawberry Kiwi Smoothie

2 kiwi, peeled and cut into chunks
1 cup frozen whole strawberries
1 container (6 ounces) strawberry nonfat yogurt
$\frac{1}{2}$ cup fat-free (skim) milk
2 tablespoons honey

1. Combine kiwi, strawberries, yogurt, milk and honey in blender or food processor; blend until smooth, pulsing to break up strawberries.

2. Pour into four glasses. Serve immediately.   *Makes 4 servings*

Soy Strawberry Kiwi Smoothie: Substitute 1 container (6 ounces) strawberry soy yogurt for regular strawberry yogurt.

Nutrients per Serving ($\frac{1}{2}$ cup): Calories: 100, Calories from Fat: 0%, Total Fat: 0g, Saturated Fat: 0g, Cholesterol: 0mg, Sodium: 45mg, Carbohydrate: 23g, Fiber: 2g, Protein: 4g

Strawberry Kiwi Smoothie

• Smoothies & More •

Frosty Raspberry Lemon Tea

1½ cups ice
  1 cup brewed lemon-flavored herbal tea, cooled to room temperature
  1 cup water
  ½ cup frozen unsweetened raspberries

1. Combine all ingredients in blender or food processor; blend until smooth, pulsing to break up ice.

2. Pour into two glasses. Serve immediately.   *Makes 2 servings*

Nutrients per Serving (1 smoothie): Calories: 14, Calories from Fat: 0%, Total Fat: 0g, Saturated Fat: <1g, Cholesterol: 0mg, Sodium: 1mg, Carbohydrate: 3g, Fiber: 1g, Protein: <1g

Sunrise Smoothie

  8 ounces frozen unsweetened peach slices, partially thawed
  8 ounces vanilla low-fat yogurt
  1 cup ice cubes
  1 can (6 ounces) pineapple juice
  2 tablespoons pourable sugar substitute*
  1 tablespoon lemon juice
  ¼ to ½ teaspoon almond extract

This recipe was tested using sucralose-based sugar substitute.

1. Combine all ingredients in blender or food processor; blend until smooth, pulsing to break up ice.

2. Pour into four glasses. Serve immediately.   *Makes 4 servings*

Nutrients per Serving (¾ cup): Calories: 99, Calories from Fat: 0%, Total Fat: 0g, Saturated Fat: 0g, Cholesterol: 3mg, Sodium: 28mg, Carbohydrate: 23g, Fiber: 1g, Protein: 2g

Frosty Raspberry Lemon Tea

Rooty Tooty Grapefruity

3 tablespoons sugar, divided
1 to 2 drops red food coloring (optional)
1 fresh ruby red grapefruit, peeled and seeded with membrane removed
1 cup crushed ice
¼ to ½ cup grapefruit juice
   Lavender or rosemary sprig (optional)

1. Tint 1 tablespoon sugar with food coloring, if desired. Moisten rims of two glasses; dip in sugar.

2. Combine grapefruit, ice, grapefruit juice and remaining 2 tablespoons sugar in blender or food processor; blend until smooth.

3. Pour into prepared glasses. Garnish with lavender sprig. Serve immediately.

Makes 2 servings

Nutrients per Serving (1 smoothie): Calories: 100, Calories from Fat: 0%, Total Fat: 0g, Saturated Fat: 0g, Cholesterol: 0mg, Sodium: 0mg, Carbohydrate: 25g, Fiber: 1g, Protein: 1g

To tint the sugar, place it in a resealable food storage bag. Add the food coloring, seal the bag and shake until sugar is evenly tinted.

Creamy Fruit Freeze

1 package (1 pound) frozen mixed fruit or peach slices, partially thawed
1 cup plain nonfat yogurt
¹/₂ cup orange juice
2 teaspoons grated fresh ginger
6 packets sugar substitute
1 teaspoon vanilla

1. Combine all ingredients in blender or food processor; blend until smooth, scraping sides frequently.

2. Pour into four glasses. Serve immediately.   *Makes 4 servings*

Nutrients per Serving (about ³/₄ cup): Calories: 106, Calories from Fat: 2%, Total Fat: <1g, Saturated Fat: <1g, Cholesterol: 1mg, Sodium: 48mg, Carbohydrate: 21g, Fiber: 2g, Protein: 5g

Chocolate Covered Banana Slushy

3 cups fat-free (skim) milk, divided
¹/₄ cup artificially sweetened chocolate instant beverage mix
1 medium banana

1. Whisk 2 cups milk and chocolate beverage mix in large measuring cup until powder dissolves. Pour chocolate milk into ice cube trays. Freeze until solid.

2. Combine chocolate ice and remaining 1 cup milk in blender or food processor. Blend until slushy, scraping sides as necessary. Add banana; blend until slushy.

3. Pour into eight glasses. Serve immediately.   *Makes 8 servings*

Nutrients per Serving (¹/₂ cup slushy): Calories: 59, Calories from Fat: 4%, Total Fat: <1g, Saturated Fat: <1g, Cholesterol: 2mg, Sodium: 66mg, Carbohydrate: 11g, Fiber: <1g, Protein: 3g

Creamy Fruit Freeze

• Smoothies & More •

Raspberry Smoothies

1¹⁄₂ cups fresh or frozen raspberries
1 cup crushed ice
1 cup plain nonfat yogurt
2 packets sugar substitute *or* equivalent of 4 teaspoons sugar
1 tablespoon honey

1. Combine raspberries, ice, yogurt, sugar substitute and honey in blender or food processor; blend until smooth.

2. Pour into four glasses. Serve immediately. *Makes 4 servings*

Nutrients per Serving (³⁄₄ cup): Calories: 80, Calories from Fat: 0%, Total Fat: 0g, Saturated Fat: 0g, Cholesterol: 0mg, Sodium: 50mg, Carbohydrate: 15g, Fiber: 3g, Protein: 4g

Mango Batido

86
calories

1 large mango, peeled, pitted and cubed
1³⁄₄ cups fat-free (skim) milk
4 ice cubes
2 tablespoons frozen orange-peach-mango juice concentrate
¹⁄₈ teaspoon almond extract (optional)

1. Combine all ingredients in blender or food processor; blend until smooth.

2. Pour into four glasses. Serve immediately.

Makes 4 servings

Nutrients per Serving (1 smoothie): Calories: 86, Calories from Fat: 3%, Total Fat: <1g, Saturated Fat: <1g, Cholesterol: 2mg, Sodium: 61mg, Carbohydrate: 18g, Fiber: 1g, Protein: 4g

Tip Chill the mango before preparing recipe or use frozen mango pieces.

Raspberry Smoothie

• Smoothies & More •

Iced Cappuccino

1 cup fat-free vanilla frozen yogurt or fat-free vanilla ice cream
1 cup cold strong brewed coffee
1 packet sugar substitute *or* equivalent of 2 teaspoons sugar
1 teaspoon unsweetened cocoa powder
1 teaspoon vanilla

1. Combine all ingredients in blender or food processor; blend until smooth. Place container in freezer; freeze 1½ to 2 hours or until top and sides of mixture are partially frozen.

2. Scrape sides of container; process until smooth and frothy.

3. Pour into two glasses. Garnish as desired. Serve immediately.

Makes 2 servings

Iced Mocha Cappuccino: Increase amount of cocoa to 1 tablespoon. Proceed as directed above.

Nutrients per Serving (1 cappuccino): Calories: 105, Calories from Fat: 0%, Total Fat: <1g, Saturated Fat: <1g, Cholesterol: <1mg, Sodium: 72mg, Carbohydrate: 21g, Fiber: 0g, Protein: 5g

Tip To add an extra flavor boost to this refreshing drink, add orange peel, lemon peel or a dash of ground cinnamon to your coffee grounds before brewing.

Iced Cappuccino

Smoothies & More

Honeydew Agua Fresca

¼ large honeydew melon, cut into small chunks and chilled
¼ cup fresh lime juice (juice of 2 limes)
2 tablespoons sugar
¼ cup fresh mint leaves
1½ cups club soda, chilled
4 to 5 lime wedges
3 to 4 mint sprigs

1. Combine melon, lime juice, sugar and mint in blender or food processor; blend until smooth. (Mixture may be blended in advance and chilled for several hours.)

2. Pour mixture into 4-cup measuring cup and stir in enough club soda to measure 4 cups.

3. Pour into four glasses. Garnish with lime wedges and mint sprigs. Serve immediately. *Makes 4 servings*

Nutrients per Serving (1 smoothie): Calories: 93, Calories from Fat: 0%, Total Fat: 0g, Saturated Fat: 0g, Cholesterol: 0mg, Sodium: 51mg, Carbohydrate: 24g, Fiber: 2g, Protein: 1g

Honeydew Agua Fresca

110 calories

•Smoothies **& More**•

Spiced Passion Fruit-Yogurt Smoothie

1 cup plain nonfat yogurt

1 cup sliced fresh strawberries

1 ripe banana, cut into pieces

¹/₄ cup frozen passion fruit juice concentrate or frozen apple-passion-mango fruit juice concentrate, thawed

³/₄ teaspoon pumpkin pie spice

¹/₈ teaspoon ground white pepper

1. Combine yogurt, strawberries, banana, juice concentrate, pumpkin pie spice and white pepper in blender or food processor; blend until smooth.

2. Pour into three glasses. Serve immediately.   *Makes 3 servings*

Nutrients per Serving (³/₄ cup): Calories: 110, Calories from Fat: 5%, Total Fat: <1g, Saturated Fat: 0g, Cholesterol: 0mg, Sodium: 65mg, Carbohydrate: 23g, Fiber: 2g, Protein: 6g

If you don't have pumpkin pie spice, you can substitute 1¹/₂ teaspoons ground cinnamon, ¹/₈ teaspoon ground ginger, ¹/₈ teaspoon ground nutmeg and a dash of ground cloves.

Spiced Passion Fruit-Yogurt Smoothie

• Smoothies **& More** •

Chocolate-Blueberry Soy Shake

$^1/_2$ **cup plus 2 tablespoons soymilk**
$^1/_4$ **cup crushed ice**
  2 tablespoons fresh or frozen blueberries (about 20 berries)
$^1/_4$ **teaspoon unsweetened cocoa powder**

1. Combine soymilk, ice, blueberries and cocoa in blender or food processor; blend until smooth.

2. Pour into chilled glass. Serve immediately. *Makes 1 serving*

Nutrients per Serving (1 shake): Calories: 99, Calories from Fat: 26%, Total Fat: 3g, Saturated Fat: <1g, Cholesterol: 0mg, Sodium: 79mg, Carbohydrate: 14g, Fiber: 2g, Protein: 5g

Honeydew Ginger Smoothie

70 calories

1$^1/_2$ cups cubed honeydew melon
$^1/_2$ **cup sliced banana**
$^1/_2$ **cup vanilla nonfat yogurt**
$^1/_2$ **cup ice cubes (about 4)**
$^1/_4$ **teaspoon grated ginger**
    Melon balls and fresh ginger slices (optional)

1. Combine honeydew, banana, yogurt, ice and ginger in blender or food processor; blend until smooth.

2. Pour into four glasses. Garnish with melon balls and ginger. Serve immediately. *Makes 4 servings*

Nutrients per Serving ($^3/_4$ cup): Calories: 70, Calories from Fat: 0%, Total Fat: 0g, Saturated Fat: 0g, Cholesterol: 0mg, Sodium: 35mg, Carbohydrate: 15g, Fiber: 1g, Protein: 2g

Chocolate-Blueberry Soy Shake

• Smoothies **& More** •

Peachy Vanilla Smoothie

1 medium peach, peeled and pitted
³/₄ cup fat-free (skim) milk
¹/₂ cup crushed ice
¹/₄ cup plain nonfat yogurt
1 tablespoon sugar substitute
¹/₄ teaspoon vanilla

1. Combine peach, milk, ice, yogurt, sugar substitute and vanilla in blender or food processor; blend until smooth.

2. Pour into two glasses. Serve immediately. *Makes 2 servings*

Nutrients per Serving (³/₄ cup): Calories: 80, Calories from Fat: 0%, Total Fat: 0g, Saturated Fat: 0g, Cholesterol: 3mg, Sodium: 60mg, Carbohydrate: 15g, Fiber: 1g, Protein: 6g

To make this smoothie more satisfying, use nonfat Greek-style yogurt, which is higher in protein than plain yogurt.

Peachy Vanilla Smoothie

● Index ●

•Index•

Metric **Conversion Chart**

VOLUME MEASUREMENTS (dry)

$1/8$ teaspoon = 0.5 mL
$1/4$ teaspoon = 1 mL
$1/2$ teaspoon = 2 mL
$3/4$ teaspoon = 4 mL
1 teaspoon = 5 mL
1 tablespoon = 15 mL
2 tablespoons = 30 mL
$1/4$ cup = 60 mL
$1/3$ cup = 75 mL
$1/2$ cup = 125 mL
$2/3$ cup = 150 mL
$3/4$ cup = 175 mL
1 cup = 250 mL
2 cups = 1 pint = 500 mL
3 cups = 750 mL
4 cups = 1 quart = 1 L

VOLUME MEASUREMENTS (fluid)

1 fluid ounce (2 tablespoons) = 30 mL
4 fluid ounces ($1/2$ cup) = 125 mL
8 fluid ounces (1 cup) = 250 mL
12 fluid ounces ($1 1/2$ cups) = 375 mL
16 fluid ounces (2 cups) = 500 mL

WEIGHTS (mass)

$1/2$ ounce = 15 g
1 ounce = 30 g
3 ounces = 90 g
4 ounces = 120 g
8 ounces = 225 g
10 ounces = 285 g
12 ounces = 360 g
16 ounces = 1 pound = 450 g

DIMENSIONS

$1/16$ inch = 2 mm
$1/8$ inch = 3 mm
$1/4$ inch = 6 mm
$1/2$ inch = 1.5 cm
$3/4$ inch = 2 cm
1 inch = 2.5 cm

OVEN TEMPERATURES

250°F = 120°C
275°F = 140°C
300°F = 150°C
325°F = 160°C
350°F = 180°C
375°F = 190°C
400°F = 200°C
425°F = 220°C
450°F = 230°C

BAKING PAN SIZES

Utensil	Size in Inches/Quarts	Metric Volume	Size in Centimeters
Baking or Cake Pan (square or rectangular)	$8 \times 8 \times 2$	2 L	$20 \times 20 \times 5$
	$9 \times 9 \times 2$	2.5 L	$23 \times 23 \times 5$
	$12 \times 8 \times 2$	3 L	$30 \times 20 \times 5$
	$13 \times 9 \times 2$	3.5 L	$33 \times 23 \times 5$
Loaf Pan	$8 \times 4 \times 3$	1.5 L	$20 \times 10 \times 7$
	$9 \times 5 \times 3$	2 L	$23 \times 13 \times 7$
Round Layer Cake Pan	$8 \times 1 1/2$	1.2 L	20×4
	$9 \times 1 1/2$	1.5 L	23×4
Pie Plate	$8 \times 1 1/4$	750 mL	20×3
	$9 \times 1 1/4$	1 L	23×3
Baking Dish or Casserole	1 quart	1 L	—
	$1 1/2$ quart	1.5 L	—
	2 quart	2 L	—